ALSO BY STEPHAN SILICH

The Silence Between What I Think and What I Say [2018]
Tonight Will be The Longest Night of Them All [2020]
Putting The Trembling Kiss at Ease [2023]
Remember Me as a Time of Day [2024]

how

impossibly

beautiful

everything

really

is

stephan silich

BROOKLYN
WRITERS PRESS

How Impossibly Beautiful Everything Really Is Copyright © 2025 Stephan Silich

All rights reserved

The Brooklyn Writers Press values and supports copyright. Copyright fuels creativity, encourages diverse voices, promotes freedom of expression, and supports a vibrant culture. Thank you for purchasing an authorized edition of this book and for respecting intellectual property laws by not reproducing, scanning, or distributing any part of it by any means without permission. You are supporting authors and enabling the Brooklyn Writers Press to continue to publish books for everyone. No part of this book may be used or reproduced in any manner for the purpose of training artificial intelligence technologies or systems.

In accordance with Article 4(3) of the Digital Single Market Directive 2019/790, the Brooklyn Writers Press expressly reserves this work from the text and data mining exception.

For permissions or information on bulk orders, please contact:
orders@bklynwriterspress.com

BROOKLYN WRITERS PRESS
An imprint of Book Biz Hub, LLC
Summit, NJ 07901

brooklynwriterspress.com

ISBNs:
978-1-952991-38-7 (eBook)
978-1-952991-39-4 (Paperback)
978-1-952991-40-0 (Hardback)

Library of Congress No. 2025902507

First Edition
Cover Photography: Stephan Silich

again…

for my daughters, emma and mia.
for my brother, robert.
for my parents, robert and dianne.

as always, this is for you.

(dad, i miss you every day, and hope you can still hear me.)

"What a precious privilege it is to be alive. To breathe, to think, to love."

Bench Plaque — Central Park, New York

contents

the clock is ticking 1

existence 10

in-between moments 11

our wounded planet 12

this old heart 14

dream 15

time 16

our hearts and our tears 17

family dinner 18

the autobiography 20

enough 22

mercy 24

a memory 25

devotion 26

new york of my soul 27

a lifetime 28

linger more, say less 29

illness 30

songs 35

life 36

pause 37

cry forever 38

phone call 39

impermanence 40

62 years 42

markers on her fingers 43

don't have a heart without music 44

the telescope 46

sunset while driving 48

a mother's love 51

sidewalk sorrows 53

move the lilacs into the sun 54

under the great stars 55

death 56

before the hours of morning 58

they may cut my candle 59

courage 60

life 63

you 64

in the late afternoon of january 65

what's next 66

the seeds and the stars 68

my broken heart 69

until the end 71

solitude 72

can we? 74

the search 77

where did they go wrong 78

54 bones in my hands 80

true artists 81

in the end 83

forget the "great things" 84

a stone to throw 86

birth 87

spread out before us 88

my job 89

your eyes 90

alone on a beach 91

making love 92

the cemetery 93

my last words 94

naked 95

holding on 96

the books and the boy 97

still in love 100

question 101

the morning light 102

an old's man life 103

1st day of work 104

splendid isolation 105

to exist 106

the ancient clouds 108

if 109

ignore it all 110

1,000 dreams 113

worthy of old age 116

the magical hand 118

father and son 119

the bird 120

win and lose 121

my sorrow is complete 122

what is success? 124

enoughness 125

before death 126

poetry 127

the story 128

fragments 129

our children 130

the human experience 134

self-worth 136

this i know to be the truth 139

silence is the experience of time passing 140

meaning 141

the music of our time 142

disregard them 143

my escape 145

what we did was love 146

when is the last time 147

presence 148

unconquerable love 149

beauty 151

fully human 153

to-do list 154

you and me 155

work 157

19-second tear drop 158

love of life 159

impermanence and presence 164

the wellspring of my heart 166

what am i going to do 167

mercy 168

heartbreak 170

gratitude 171

try 173

the one 174

sleep 175

love 177

the resilience of life 178

these flowers 179

lyrics and words 180

blessings 183

stars at night and our fragile hearts 184

until the rest of mine 187

live 188

i miss you dad and thank you mom 189

10 questions to ask 192

these bones are aching 193

just us 195

we are made of stars 196

winter 197

existence 199

hope 200

the ancient trees 201

the beautiful small near misses 202

the sound 203

122 east 76th street, 4th floor 204

the staggering privilege to live is ours 211

how impossibly beautiful everything really is 213

postscript 215

For My Dad

About My Dad

acknowlegements

About the Author

the clock is ticking
a commencement speech, a manifesto, a small book, some advice, some thoughts…

these words are my version of life, nothing more, nothing less.

i know the clock is ticking and that is the greatest gift ever given. if you know this and live it, life can be wonderful.

the life of your heart is all you need to know. I have been living with mortality since I was 16 years old when I saw a mother decapitated from a car accident in front of her husband and 2 young daughters, age 7 and 5. it changed everything.

i say to myself every day, wouldn't life be magnificent if everyone was threatened with death at any moment? we are humans, and death can come this morning, this afternoon, this evening.

life is simply the art of presence. this is our fortune. and this is often most difficult living in New York City where everyone is in a rush, clocking their productivity, running to meet their goals, calculating their metrics, powerwalking through their days, past each other, past the buildings, the trees, the birds, even their true loves. which all leads to unlived and unremembered lives.

have no ambition for the things that the world tells you to worship. there is a sacred dimension to every minute and to our human existence. it is the haunting reminder of time; each laugh may be the last laugh; each parting may be the last parting.

all of us will go through life together, loving and losing all we have and all we love, and that is one of our deepest sources of communion.

we need to unravel the unseen and unheard miracles of each day. we need to examine the details of the ordinary, touch the fabric of experience, and embrace the impermanence. it is the grandeur of life, humble and magical at the same time.

it is always celebration over lamentation where the radiant sunrise is the city's warm embrace, blazing with light through carnage and chaos, joy and jubilation. moments seared into our memories until our last days. memories from poetic observations and contemplative reflections.

look down and see the restless leaf that fell and sank onto the wet concrete at just the right moment. feel the small hand of your child inside your hand as you walk to school. smell the pine in the gentle wind across park avenue. touch the earth if you can find a patch of soil. listen to the birdsong all around you. watch the shifting clouds above. take in the museum entrance, the music in the early morning, the books holding each other on your shelf, the sidewalk chalk drawings of children, and the warmth of the sun on your face on a winter's day.

it is the art of seeing. and it is the distinguishing art of seeing the captivating elegance and splendor of life.

have awe for every single thing that is alive. awe is the beautiful absence of self. keep it close. notice all the splendidness so you see the whole and the specific minutes that should go by without scheduled activities or intended tasks. grow your hair long if you want and fill your garden with sunflowers if you can. watch the light shimmer across the surface of your coffee cup.

give in to the fascination. keep looking for the things that make you marvel.

recapture the wonder of childhood. it is the art of noticing that is the secret to a child's mind.

stay in the now of something vast and breathless. it can be part of everyday life. it will cause your heartbeat to slow and your breath to deepen. it most certainly will never require privilege or wealth, vacations to faraway places, or any other material status symbol. it is everywhere if you are present to take it in.

how often do you pause to appreciate the bounty that is upon us?

everything is poetry, and all poetry is found in the hearts of humanity. listen to the silence. allow yourself to be fragile. the sensitive ones teach us that hope is always in the shadows. and the sensitive ones will thankfully have the hardest time as they listen, give attention, stand ready to take on someone's pain, and are always willing to give warmth at any cost.

life is the survival of the kindest.

the present is filled with more mystery, more magnificence, and more memories held together by the early evening twilight with astonishing courage and steadfastness against the opposite view that would bring most people to their knees.

fight minute by minute, hour by hour, and day by day for the precious present.

we get a single chance at survival, so don't regret who you haven't become, don't find meaning in what's never happened, don't imagine unlived lives, don't be haunted by the life you might have led.

don't linger longer and say more. sink deeper into the life you have, value who you are now. life requires time, thought, and contemplation to fully perceive it. all of it requires an astounding patience.

keep your willingness to embrace uncertainty and make peace with the unresolved.

choose life over work because who you are and what you do for a living are two very different things. what we should do and what we can do are also two very different things. your time is finite, and at the end of it all, you should be remembered for who you were, and not what you did for a living.

disregard the worshiping of success, the obsession with titles, ratings and rankings, the fear of failure, the horror of losing. forget the meaningless ladders of achievement where all others are left behind. it is a merciless and destructive, competitive life.

work is not a virtue, despite witnessing everyone sacrifice almost everything in the name of that next promotion, the next raise. graduate degrees do not bestow wisdom and performance goals do not equate to dignity.

disregard the description of success and remember that success usually illuminates a person's faults anyway, so you will dislike them even more if you disliked them before they were successful.

and what is success anyway? look at the vanity, the quest for money, the ones who want to be noticed with their desperate need

to rise above the crowd. this behavior only adds to the cruelties of daily life.

give, don't take, and the more you give, the more riches you will find in yourself.

money is a corrupting force and few who pursue it relentlessly do so without grave damage to themselves and others, and few do so without compromising their character and well-being.

remain unmoved by recognition.

be prepared to work without applause.

learn the importance of slowing down in a world that demands speed.

disregard the constant appetite for the new, the hyped and overexposed, the flashy and the false, the reinvented and the reformulated.

the person who wants the least is the person who will have the most.

it is the off-center, in-between state that is the tenderest of life. stay tender. when you wake each morning, it is your time to begin to exist. to become deeply human, keep attunement to nature and to all humanity.

have a profound kindness to everything that exists.

forget the "if only" mind that haunts us all. stay focused on bursting with the great joys and terrible sorrows.

go with the bittersweet. balance your despair with serenity. anchor yourself in the now. have the fortitude to hold it all in your heart.

let the music of your unspeakable emotions fill you with

uncommon beauty and uncommon terror. live with blushing brilliance like the tender-winged birds at the mercy of every breeze.

know what it means to have the right heart and the enduring enchantment of all that is wonderous in this life.

feel the pulse of other people's pain and know the sacredness of grief.

be able to sit alone with staggering silence, honoring unresolved loss and the ongoing shadows of life. in the face of this impermanence, it takes braveness to love the things that will slip through both of your hands at the end. live your life and your choices.

draw your own portrait. write your own poem. sing your own song.
become your life's work of art.

your real life is richer than you think. there is a light within us from birth to death, so forget the unsaid, the unseen, and the unlived. the absolute present is all we have, and this realization expands possibility. the here and now is something remarkable.

life will not be easy, and none of it is definite, but there is hope. the essential role of hope, anchored beyond the horizon.

and as you live majestically, moving through the stages, meet each person on their own terms, and that will be the supreme art of living. spend time slowing down, and you will realize that the answer is always in the attempt, in the effort, and in the trying.

if a quiet anguish arrives, do not allow a flatness to your voice, do not allow a stillness in your eyes. the inevitability of aging, with our wrong paths, failed dreams, terrible choices, and bad chapters, will provide us the divine delicacy of incompleteness.

create something, but go beyond art. go into life itself. acknowledge the glimpses of love, and if you peer into darkness, you can still find joy. stay awake to these times.

take life by the hand, with both hands gently, and give her solace because you will know how profound and lasting the inner aches can be. wrap your arms around these moments of dignified hope, awareness, openness, discernment, limitlessness, exuberance, and lightness - the lightness of life.

live the fullness of your humanity, and you may be remembered as music, or as a time of day. let all your words become your sweetest songs. breathe in the midst of uncertainty, learning

never to panic. stay wondrously vibrant and blazing with the same joys and agonies.

have the devotion to make life's invisible visible.

see everything through fresh eyes, gentleness of tone, and the reassuring kindness of your manner. live with a broken heart if you have to. don't run from it. don't try to fix it.

the wakefulness to all of life will allow the things you care for to continue after you are gone, like the trees you planted knowing you will never sit in their shade. this will honor the unfolding of time.

step forward a little further.

what made you a bit different as a child will make you a spectacular human being as an adult.

be thoughtful and caring about how people are doing and how your very being and actions affect them. don't try and make the pain go away. in moments of despair, make a quiet friend of life, embrace it with your deepest self, fighting through the difficult and beautiful truths of life.

dismantle the old ways of seeing, touching, hearing, smelling, and tasting.

witness the goodness of others. search to see them doing small gestures, like walking the elderly across the street, paying attention to your neighborhood bus driver, or thanking the grocery clerk.

let the birds and flowers, the vast forests, and the glittering sea, inspire you. plunge yourself into nature over and over and over again. look skyward to draw us closer together by our mutual smallness against the immensity of this galaxy.

stay awake and do not be blindfolded to wonder. keep your curiosity and extend a helping hand full of goodwill to someone else's struggle.

life is everywhere.

the blooming of lilacs occurs every day. let it unfold on you.

the best way to find something is not to go looking for it.

admit your love. express your love. let it echo through generations.

there may be some agony in finding everyday happiness, but this is the architecture of character. these are your moments of strength and endurance.

things are always in transition. always changing.

letting go will be the heartbeat of all things.

whatever happens is not the beginning nor the end.

it is the start.

it is the small acts of hope like a weighted blanket of quiet.

a reassuring hush.

a whisper.

and if not much time remains, then I can only hope these words are a worthy and noble farewell.

live, don't just last.

I love you.

existence

we speak of love until nightfall
under the living monuments of trees.

it reminds me of the mystery of existence,
our faint distant galaxies
floating into view from all generations of life,
from here to almost infinity and back.

our familiar touch will always be there,
even in our last moments together.

we will stand together at eternity's gate.

the eventual absence may seem
to drain the magic,
but if you allow time to befriend you,
the amazement will endure,
especially if you turn toward it
and rise to the boundless sky between us.

in-between moments

sometimes, at night,
or early in the morning,
i can hear the birds sing.

i remember quiet things, like
how the wind seems softer,
the evening stars brighter,
mountains and rivers holding hands,
sunsets and moonlight
whispering to each other,
and a glimpse of the sea,
and a breeze off the water.
i stand still
to take this all in.

i find peace always
in these remarkable
in-between moments.

our wounded planet

this was our benevolent planet,
which gave us nothing but nourishment,
and yet we gravely wound
the exact thing that loves us.

and here we are, damaged,
with an undercurrent of sadness
running through it all,
but still slowly drifting to you
as you crack open the vast capacity for light
to see this day with equal parts
benevolence and astonishment.

you are our poem, our love letter,
our elegy, our long-awaited eulogy.

a single human being
a humble life
love overflowing
living proof of the human need to be chosen.

and you were chosen, and this is our moment,
our rare moment of peace, of quiet,
and of reflection.

it is the things we see, the people we touch,
the emotions we feel.

it is the scent of a flower we have not yet smelled.
it is the echo of a song we have not yet heard.

let's remain lucidly aware of the miracles
that surround us and with the here and now.

the unfolding of time

the sacred and the profane

the humanities and the vulnerabilities

the triumphs and the failures,

and the countless sleepless nights
that remind us that it is how we treat each other
in the smallest acts of daily life that matter most.

this old heart

there
will
always
be
a
place
in
this
old
heart
for
you.

dream

when night
pulls down the sun,
i dream of you
while everyone else sleeps.

time

all times of silence have a purpose

a time of patient expectation,
of hopeful waiting,
of already and not yet.

possibilities refusing
to be constrained by convention.

warm and full of love for one another,
with heartache besieged.

the discovery of touch
brings something resonant and true.

it will be the ordinary times
spent together through the years
that speak to life's most essential memories.

setting the table,
lighting the candles,
burning the fire,
brushing your hair,
holding your hand.

in the hush of not-yet-dawn,
i realize there is so much bravery
in trying,
and sometimes failing,
but always trying again.

our hearts and our tears

be gentle as time passes us by.

our hearts will be broken,
but we do not have to break with them.

everything is briefly wonderful,
so hold every heart with both hands
to honor the unfolding of time,
which remains permanently
imprinted on our souls.

let life live itself through you,
moment by moment.

the immensely delicate loving,
with the inevitability of losing the chosen few,
will bring sorrow and pain of unbearable proportions,
leaving in our wake stars dimmed by our tears.

but between requiem and redemption,
all of life will flow through us
as our eyes look ahead in the same direction
and then face-to-face with thoughtful reflections
on what it means to be human with an expressed love
that will stay with us until our last days.

family dinner

my ex-wife and i decided early on to be very peaceful
and loving and keep our family together in any way we could,

she always said we failed as a married couple
but succeeded as friends and loving parents.

as we walk through these new times,
maybe we can show up for each other
with kindness and compassion.

and so we have family dinners every wednesday night
with our 2 beautiful daughters.

through the disarray of all the separation,
this still is my surest source of strength
in an indifferent world.

what they don't know and what i hide from them
is that my emotions are always simmering
just below the surface of every minute of each day,
especially between all that i feel
and all that can't be easily said.

they don't know that as soon as i
walk out of her apartment,
i weep into the night.
and i can't fall asleep.
and i can't rest my head.

but in my dreams, i see you.
in my heart i still feel you.

and in my waking life, i try to remain alive
with a fervent soul that's just for you.
everything i do is all for you.

everything is always for you.

i know that mourning is not some process
we are to endure until life restores itself.

life continues with or without our consent,
so i build all the love
into the daily patterns of my life.

we even get together for holidays and vacations,
and they don't know that during these special times
i excuse myself very often with
"i need some fresh air"
or "i have to go to the bathroom,"
and i walk alone weeping and weeping
that we are not a family in the traditional sense.
i've learned to hide it well.

but i make this a sacred place for myself,
and it's very delicate,
and i allow these nights to soften my eyes,
and i am able to allow the memories
to hold me close when i'm tired.

i can look out my window
and sometimes see the rising moon,
and it reminds me of how
improbably lucky we still all are.

this is the night-light we need.

and this is the grace
that dissolves the edges of tomorrow,
making for a new day
where i wake and start anew
and keep trying
and keep loving as much as i possibly can.

the autobiography

let the blood drip from pen to paper
as you write the autobiography of your heart.

live above the human equations.

explode with hope.

melt into the ocean of time.

burn life's anguish.

paint the brushstrokes of the sun.

sing the songs of the sea.

listen to the symphony of the birds.

keep the air void of lamentations.

shout the voices of humanity.

dream your dream.

cry your tears.

and live and love in a world apart.

the painted flowers of grief

the tortured irises of van gogh,
his painted flowers of grief,
don't seem to ever fade.

death is certainly
not the only occasion for sadness.

the reasons are many,
and you may have to squint a little to see it
as the loss and absence is always there,
but maybe this can be the comfort
that holds us together.

our bereavement is our ability to love,

and our love will turn
flowers into meaning
and sorrow into song.

enough

at some point
i will become
a little discouraged
as i face the long sleep,
but my life will stay with you
and hopefully felt by you.

i will do everything i can
so that you will remember me.

i hope you find me.

i hope i remain here
through all the feelings that are
irrepressible and uncontainable,

through all of your childhood confusions
and desolations,

through the triumphs and victories,

through the grief and suffering,

through the delight and elation.

let me move from occupying your thoughts
to residing comfortably in your hearts.

with time and with thought
and with the remembrance
that i am still overwhelmed by the grace
by which you live and love your life.

this is enough.

it was always enough.

mercy

sing me a tender ballad,
with sorrow undivided.

make me golden again.
make me part of your dream.

we can't get back the stone after it's thrown,
the words after they're said,
the time after it's gone.

i ask for mercy for the unremembered
failures of a lifetime
and continue searching earnestly
for the meaning in
the turbulence of thought,
the quickening of the heart,
and the opening of possibility.

in every unimaginably difficult story,
there is always a single ray of sunlight
that will make its way through.

a memory

i study this life
without appearing to be a part of it.

shuddering with disbelief,
i am crestfallen under a sky
trembling with stars that remain eternal,
offering a brief glimpse of what is sacred.

i will discreetly brush away the tears
with these fading memories,

but i will make another memory,
that i am sure of,
and you, my love,
will be the memory that lasts.

devotion

i am listening
to the dream
you wove today
as the sun goes down
and your faces fill the sky
full of stars.

i shelter here some days,
alone with these thoughts.

you're the ones that i always miss.

please play the songs
we used to sing together.

take your time coming home,
but hurry up.

you light the path
that brings the arrival of a new day.

i am alone at the moment,
but i am right behind you,
close enough to kiss your cheeks,
close enough to reach for your hands.

like a snapshot,
or a passing ripple of time,
it all makes me realize that
everything is ephemeral,
but because of you
and this life still to live,
you will always get my total devotion.

new york of my soul

i remember coming out of work,
into the night,
and heading home to my apartment.

the best moment for me was the walk
because this city
is where i complete the search
with a little love,
a bit of conversation,
some decent food,
a few glasses of wine,
and time to remember.

that's all.
just time to remember.

it was such easy luck that came my way.

a lifetime

i ask sorrow to let me rest
since rest is all i have.

for once i was,
and here,
in heart,
i always will be.

accepting the truth of this hour,
i will let the serenity we are given
fight despair and protect our feelings.

abandoned we will feel,
yet suffer most in order to heal.

a lifetime it will seem,
but a lifetime we will live,

and it's a lifetime always
as real as the poet's promise.

linger more, say less

i hurried downtown
where the brightness of you was waiting.

i never counted on loving you so much
because i always found meaning
in what never happened
and in the life unlived.

the divine discontent
led me to live
apart from our time,
dwelling in the margins of books
and in the margins of life.

now there is you
and this story
that make me linger more and say less
among the carelessness of our passing youth.

it's only the unfinished complications
that make us human as we live through
this single shot of our unbearable existence.

illness

illness steals away the certainties
and our gentle insistence on permanence,
vanquishing our sense of invincibility,
but if we look past the labored breaths
and aching silence,
we can celebrate the essence
and the ceremonies of farewell.

every moment now has emotional weight,
but there is always
a beacon of hope in the distance.

the acceptance of our vulnerability
and that we need care throughout our lives
will enable us to live with compassion
and heart-healing kindness.

it is the possibility of the impossible.

it is the requiem of the saved.

if my breath is taken from me before my time,
i leave you both in the hands of the world,
with your young lives still unwritten,
waiting to be colored in with living.

and live you will.
you will go with the life of warmth,
you will go with the inclinations of your heart,
you will search for truth and for meaning
and for a way to live with your human fragility.

you will follow the benevolent light.
it will be there for you always,
i promise.

and when the clouds suspend all thought,
every face will become a memory.

the stunning sunset aglow outside
will be the look in my eye,
and all the tender notes
will be my voice whispering to you both.

from everywhere, all at once

happiness lies in the most ordinary of moments

a quiet taking of the hand
a kind word
a warm smile.

the enduring value of this is right here,
in the passing moments.

the most precious affirmation of endurance
is the humble grace of our lives.

it is how we fill this life
with our living moments of meaning.

i beg you not to forget that i never,
not for a single moment,
doubted your love for me.

i love you too,
and that love reverberates across the universe,
past a thousand suns and through ancient galaxies,
emanating from everywhere all at once.

i think of you now and weep with happiness.

and i weep again now, writing this down.

let's let the angels endure
with wisdom and warmth,
both timeless and timely.

these are the golden hours of our lives,
always growing with a sense
of this beautiful pure feeling of love.

what survives

we are, as human beings,
the poems of something greater than us.

standing here with echoes of joy and agony,
waiting with edgeless love to tell our story
that up until now remained untold.

it is important because our words
will hopefully survive
with shades of brilliance
through flesh and bone,
and revelation and reticence

becoming the emblem of
our reservoir of promise,
our capacity for hope,
and our sense of sacredness.

we know that at the heart
of the human condition
are our softly exchanged words,
dripping with emotion,
and an exhilarated sense of awe
about the possibilities
still left in nature.

part of that is the ability
to pay attention to the most ordinary things
and understand how extraordinary they really are.

sometimes what people need
is immediate forgiveness,
and that show of kindness and mercy
can alter the path of a person's life.

these are the days we live,
where death is not in the background.

sit still now.

stay with silence.

don't do anything.

sometimes being productive

is the surest way to distract yourself from living.

please don't mistake doing for being.

catch a glimpse of this as it all passes by.

join me with suffocating sensitivity
that marks our daily life,
rushing through the cracks of each day.

and remember that each day
you are devoting yourself
to someone or something,
may very well be your last.

it is simply the enduring urgency of today
and what it means to live well in one's soul.

songs

when words fail,
as they often do,
there is always music.

with the right songs,
you will either remember everything
or forget everything.

in between the singing,
i will give you the same
aching stillness i give myself.

let this soften your eyes
and quiet your mind,
because you have already
lived a lifetime in your youth.

remember,
the medications never work;
they just injure your nervous system,
and you will find the staggering joy
that waits at the edges of every sorrow.

the answer to the question of life
is to live now.

and although what remains
will be old and worn,
it will still be beautiful.

life

being reunited.

rain on rooftops.

the first sip of wine.

music in the background.

stories we can't tell fast enough.

the celebration of contentment.

unimaginable forgiveness.

the determination to walk away.

the delicacy of your words.

living a full life unseen.

long nights of reading and serenity.

the laying of hands at the heart of prayer rituals.

reclaimed connections, lost from childhood.

the strength of patience.

the moment we choose to remember.

and the holding on for the last time,
before letting it all slip away, quietly.

pause

our stardust is swirling,
but we have stopped
for a moment to love each other.

we live under the immense,
incalculable blue skies.

we live, thankfully,
quietly and unknown.

we experience joy
with tears in our eyes.

we experience beauty
by letting go of our expectations.

i hold you close,
like a memory,
and will love you exuberantly
because you stopped me from blinking.

ask yourself who you are?

what do you really stand for?

what have you done for our planet?

how do you wish to be remembered?

all i know
is the refracted light of your love
and its urgent immediacy,
which lay incessantly on my heart,
is all i ever need.

cry forever
mia silich, 7-years-old [january 6, 2023]

putting mia to sleep,
gathering her stuffed animals,
her lavender blanket,
her cup of water with extra ice.
tucked her in,
kissed her cheek,
and gave her a hug.

when she pulls me close, she says:

> *"daddy, i just realized*
> *that grandpa was to you*
> *what you are to me.*
> *you must be so sad your dad died,*
> *because if you die*
> *i will cry forever.*
> *every day.*
> *every night.*
> *forever and ever."*

thank you, mia.

it was at that moment
that i realized childhood
is both a time and a place.

the fluttering of my heart
as i stared at another delicate heart
with astounding sensitivity,
arrived with the timeless
replaying of sweet memories
and a certain endlessness
for our everlasting love.

phone call

when i received the phone call
that my dad had died
i was walking to work
listening to music
and the song was *"love is all."*

> *"steve, dad just died. i'm so, so sorry. i love you.*
> *i love you so much. i promise you it will be ok.*
> *i'm always here for you…"*

that's all i remember
from my brother's beautiful voice.

and then i returned to the music,
listening to the lyrics of the song,
which sang about breezes carrying us
softly in the air
and learning how
to breathe easy.

impermanence
(the wave)

i am staring at the vast, still ocean,
and i know the planets will soon shift.

the tides will pull,
the moon will strengthen,
and from this i know a wave
will start to form somewhere,
and the planet will continue to turn.

the tides will carry on under the arms of the moon,
and the wave will rise and fall again,
and the ocean will be still once more.

all around us stars are born,
birthing new solar systems
full of planets and moons.
and the oceans will remain,
and we will remain.

i may look like a normal person,
but i don't live like anyone else.

my heart feels different.

i have found a way to walk through this life.

i have found a way to garden through the winter.

i have emerged undiminished and revitalized
and let the experiences of the day race through me
so i can reach my night of solace
with you in my arms,
forever, like the wave that rises and falls
but is always there.

always part of the ocean,
always waiting,
always continuing.

the transformation of my human heart
will now be complete.

62 years

thank you
to my parents
who were together
in love
for 62 years.

i was given a clear definition of love
early in life that made me
a much more loving person.

like the rapture of first love,
you take the air right out of my lungs.

i realize now i have spent most of my life
trying to recover what had been lost…

to return to my first home
and the belief in the sacredness
of love's promise.

markers on her fingers
for emma

emma climbs into my bed at 4:30am
and puts her arms around me.

i take her hand in mine
and run my fingers over hers
and notice the faded stains
of pink paint and purple markers
that didn't wash off in the bath.

it makes me cry for some reason.

i am alone with silence,
the lump in my throat,
and the fullness in my chest.

this is the divine state of humanity,
and i will listen closely
and hear nothing but the echo of love's
declaration of eternity.

i will watch you always,
as you take this world
into your growing heart
and live with the sun by day
and the stars by night.

don't have a heart without music

the grief is real
because the love is real.

what originates in sadness
can be transformed into joy
and the healing art of continuing.

grief means you remember.

no love is ever wasted,
and no grief is either.

the memory of the life lived
and the love given will exist
even through the brokenness
that the wounds created.

the love we pour into each other remains.

it turns the ephemeral into something permanent,

the mortal into something eternal.

it is how we manage to open our eyes
the next morning when our beloved is gone,

still haunted by the fact that everyone disappears.

love is the only gift in life that is never lost.

and i am overwhelmed by what is left,
by what unfolds,
by what endures,
by what remains.

today, and each day,
is always the right day for love.

the telescope
for mia

for my youngest daughter's 7th birthday,
she asked for a telescope to look more closely
at the stars and the moon.

what can be more beautiful?

for thousands of years,
humans have carved stars into rocks
and painted constellations on cave walls.

we've been looking up to find ourselves
since the beginning of time.

we still don't have the answers,
but not knowing becomes the intimacy
with ourselves and our life.

we sit together
in this state of not knowing
and somehow find a way to rest here,
and that makes all the difference.

we sit and rest
and take whatever life has to offer
and give back an infinite amount more.

it is why i write these words
and leave you these books.

i am hopeful that poetry is noticing
what is ordinarily unnoticed.

it is the shiver of awareness.

it is that which is not contained.

it is life with its complete fullness.

it is love will all its sufficiency.

these words are nothing more than
the evidence of my time here.

i carve them into stone for you

and hopefully leave a permanent whisper
for you to hear always.

touchingly,
tragically,
they are my love letters
to the stars
and to you both,

and the only way
i know how to make the tender moments
of this one and only life worth living.

sunset while driving
sunday, march 5, 2023 5:30pm

driving west to manhattan
from springs, east hampton,
nature started to do her thing
at the approach of twilight.

music on,
sun piercing our windows
with the orange glow
glittering everything
and everyone.

we are awakened to the miracle of life
as we get to experience this sky,
these clouds,
these colors,
these loves of mine in this car.

i'm writing this poem in my head as i drive.

most people don't want to sit
in their cars,
on buses,
on trains,
or on planes,
waiting,
but this works very well for me.

i've always found great stillness
in the midst of the busyness
and distractions of life.

ask yourself now, how do you spend
the hours,
the minutes,

the seconds of life?

i'm lucky enough to be here spending mine
wrapped in this experience
of being a father
and navigating these feelings.

i breathe the air,
drink the water,

and live in each season as it passes,
resigning myself to the magic of awe and wonder.

i worry still that careless human beings
continue to be careless
with their fixation on control,
their fixation on accumulation,
their view of nature as a resource to be extracted,
their resistance to disintegration and impermanence.

life is disproportionate and inherently unfair
and carries on with or without our consent.

this makes life devastating,
but it is also enchanting.

we live in a time of grace
but also a time of horror.

we need to see more clearly and truly,
feel more deeply and delicately.

we need to learn to love
being alive for the moment we are here
in this immense span of time.

hold the fragility of everything we have made.

take more of the unseen and bow in its direction.

listen for the first bird of morning,

and be continuous with those
we love because the slightly broken
will always love more tenderly.

a mother's love
for mom — dianne silich

trusting our shared heartbeats
aglow with shimmering feelings.

solitary, but never alone.

it is still a living struggle,
day after day,
waiting for a grain of hope,
searching for a spark of love.

we don't know where this life will lead,
and a great deal of time passes
as we crawl through the days
sinking into flowerbeds
until we reach for the fullness
of life that is possible.

these very human hands touch our skin
as our bones tremble and shiver
and humanity breaks into a million pieces,
dimming the stars at night.

but these faint lights will remain
and will always be here,
like a mother's love.

against this symphony of time
and beneath the daily task of living,
we know that by falling again and again,
we learn to walk.

i am alive because of you.

your breath for sound.

your hands for touch.

i ask myself:
will i remember what it feels
like to be this alive?

it fills me with burning suns
as the glory of the human condition
makes its way through the day unscathed,

but not untouched.

how do i still help people feel less alone?

how do i live a little warmer?

perhaps with an honesty
that will move some to tears
as i search for those great words
in the shadow of the sun.

i know that between night and nothingness,
there is always you,
the lens on the miraculous wonder of life.

you are every book i ever read,
every dream i ever dreamt,
and every love i ever loved.

sidewalk sorrows

walking down sun-bleached sidewalks
worrying about the rent
and the next bottle of wine.

learning to laugh through tears
and live without cliches
as everyone else looks coldly on life
and accepts mediocrity
as if it's some sort of necessity.

after watching an old man
sell potted plants in the street,
we return home to notice the dog
hiding alone under the chair.

and it's the weight of living
that is bewildering and unknowable
as we move through the seasons
with the wistfulness of loss.

we watch leaves fall to the ground
but continue living with grace,
knowing that the purest solace
is in the privilege of loving.

move the lilacs into the sun

i walk among the aging apartments
and occasionally stop to flip through the
thumb-stained pages of the ones who came before me.

i think of you still when the brave sun
shimmers over low clouds,
and i have nowhere to stand but in this poem.

i will remain here while
teenagers crash on the highway,
women meet over cups of tea,
men pick fruit in open fields,
and poets rest under beech trees.

it is time
to return to my dreams.

it is time
to move the lilacs into the sun.

and it is time
to strengthen myself with silence
equal to the importance of any words.

and because of this,
these words must now become silent.

under the great stars

on this restless summer night,
i sit under the great stars
as the universe sighs before me.

i watch this night unfold
as if watching someone i love sleeping,
and i wonder what would i do
if she were here with me.

though she is far away
and in the arms of another,
i will sit here still
with my thoughts of her,
and nothing will fade this moment.

death

listen to the drowning man
and see how death trembles us all.

but death will still remain:

the broken shoelace,
the busy signal,
the runway model,
the drunk landlord,
the 9 to 5,
the last piece of toilet paper,
the shiny blond weatherman,
the preening actor,
the strip club,
the presidential vote,
the celebrity interview,
the controlling boss,
and the false laughter
at the cocktail party
and all that goes with it.

so, hear us scream,
listen to us weep,
and witness the suffering
of a lifetime on our faces.

but as the years pass,
life after life
age after age,
we won't let distance
slowly form between us,
and we won't let life
pull us in different directions.

there may be more beautiful times,

but this one is ours.

we will find the light in each other
that we couldn't find in others
after all those years of unspent love.

before the hours of morning

this feeling of watching everything pass
and everyone disappear is exquisitely haunting
and often seems that before we even have a moment
to capture the beauty of it all,
it's already slipping away.

i will spend some time now
tracing the letters on your gravestone.

but i will always have
my mother kissing my sleepy eyes goodnight,
my father steadying my bicycle,
my brother straightening my necktie,
and my daughters' outstretched arms
hugging me goodnight.

this comfort is always
sketched on the night's sky,
even before the hours of morning.

they may cut my candle

avoid the coffeehouse attitudes,
and in the shadows of archways
you will find the hummingbird
singing for you.

let me pass you on the street
and get that feeling again
for a brief moment.

let my lungs fill with unspecific tragedy
because life hides from so many of us,
and not everyone seeks a safe and scripted life.

give me this
and the wind
and the ocean-driven sea,
and i will bathe in this dim light of truth
as the old man bids farewell
under grey clouds on an unseasonably warm day.

courage

the courage to know yourself.

keeping my brown eyes shining with tears,
opening those same eyes
to the unending vastness of it all,
staying openhearted and kind,
calm during chaos,
comfortable with uncertainty,
seeing others with value and dignity,
radiating warmth through the art
of being here in full awareness,
looking for meaning that clarifies truth,
and the joy of seeing grace anew in us both.

then there are the broken relationships,
personal failures, work betrayals,
dishonorable bosses, maneuvering colleagues,
apathetic and opportunistic,
but it all comes with the
vulnerability of getting older,
because life has a way of making you
more tender as you age.

i have seen things people wouldn't believe,
things that still leave my pillow tearstained nightly.

yet in the sweep of human history,
i have also seen love that staggers me awake.

these experiences shape your identity,
and your understanding continues
through memory, cultivated with a little solitude.

you can live with wholeheartedness
and vulnerability.

you can walk straight into your not knowing
so you can live also with some brokenness,
have a lived life full of falling down
and getting back up.

we all want our work to make a difference,
but it certainly won't be during the hours of 9-5.

there is work much more important,

like the spread of love and kindness
that is within your reach,
and attending to the true needs of those
entrusted in your care.

let this pierce your heart
with its joys and griefs,
and let your heart break open,
but not apart.

try this and your eyes will focus
on the astounding grandeur of life.

let humanity be continuous and unified.

what matters is what you add to your human story.

know that your time
wasn't easier than ours,
because no time can be easier
if you are living through it.

just keep the emptiness out of your eyes
and the dust from your hearts,

and like a fragile flower,

with delicate attention
find your love
and let it remain
undiminished by time.

life

life sweeps us off our feet
and sometimes brings us to our knees

by a diagnosis that arrives
on a tuesday afternoon,

an opportunity that emerges
over a morning coffee,

or a beautiful person that
quietly enters your heart.

and then you must begin again,
enhancing the way you live your life,
holding on to the immense depth of each moment,
and understanding that compassion arises
from the same place where all harmony blooms.

you

the most memorable part for me is you,
so sing me a simple song,
pick me a little flower,
light a match for the candle,
tear a page from your love letter.

when you whisper my name,
i hear all that is left behind.

i gasp in grateful incomprehension
for the irreplaceable symphony of our songs.

i look past the chorus of anguish,
and my heart illuminates what it means
to be human with magnified resolve.

out of this bewilderment,
our poetry must come and stay bearable
across the essential impermanence of life.

because if i could turn back time,
i would have met you much sooner
and loved you much longer.

but i will find you again,
in every lifetime.

in the late afternoon of january

i feel so much better looking at you,
and it's nice to feel this way,
especially when you know it's the little things:

the glimpse of your dazzling eyes
briefly catching mine,
or the way your hair falls
to the sides of your shoulders.

you are my beautiful accident,
the one i dreamed of, but never expected,
and it almost broke me
before our beautiful beginning.

but even your absence
fills the empty spaces of night,
like the sun exposing herself
for a brief moment
in the late afternoon of january.

what's next

everything you need is right in front of you,
so live with intention, no matter your daily ritual.

look for moments of radiance.

embrace people, not things.

nothing has to be newer, younger, shinier.

celebrate living for the smaller reasons.

live with more hope and less fear.

let kindness prevail once and for all.

possess less to have more.

the latest and most urgent is not the most important.

listen to understand and not just to reply.

amongst all the immensities and possibilities,
reflect on the fragility of life.

disregard spending and owning
to demonstrate one's wealth and status.

take responsibility for the air you breathe
and the space you inhabit.

deliberately distance yourself
from theinessential things.

be eloquent with life,
and especially with love,

for love will always remain
the naked flower waiting to unfold.

the seeds and the stars

in the history of our life,
between the seeds below
and the stars above,
amid a world so readily given to despair,
you can still cycle through the seasons
knowing that love takes time and due care.

squinting into the sun
to see the haunting nature of our mortality.

tenderness and kindness
are life's enduring source of meaning.

take the long view,
and have a lived sense of what is most important.

wrap your arms around the tragedies and the triumphs.

bind your feelings of your lifetime,
weave them together
with no abatement of substance.

stay present,
never detached;
never be finished with life,
and always surrender to the sweep of love.

my broken heart

my broken heart is weary,
but the sorrow will not blur
my perception of time and space.

you have left behind
one last serene note of farewell.

how will i describe the state of my being now?

how will i remain a human being?

through these unanswerable moments,
i learn how to pay attention to the light
and the dark this world gives us.

life and art is the inheritance of all of us
to honor and carry across these moments
when our lives are shimmering on the edges.

how is that so many people can ignore
suffering as much as they do?

cry with me
at our hope,
at our time,
at our life.

who is the person staring back at us from the mirror?

we will carry these years in our bodies and on our faces.

but together now,
on the verge,
and on the cusp,
we can fully live
with our deepest state of love.

until the end

tell me what you hold inside.

let me touch the map of your skin.

we don't have much time.

we are getting older,
but we have each other
right now.

we have the remembering
of the lives we have lived.

we can still make plans.
we can still make vows.
we can still have the shape of love
remain undiminished by the passing of time.

we have the inextinguishable enormity
of our togetherness
and our eternal longing for home.

i will follow you everywhere,
and i will stay with you until the very end.

solitude

it has been a full and contented life
with no visitations of great loneliness
or deafening circumstances.

and the few concerns that arrived
only served as a gentle reminder
to stay present with gratitude.

despite some lacerations to the soul,
i was granted many prolonged,
peaceful nights and moments of pure solitude.

the generosity of aloneness,
and the gloriousness of time
is the reminder that the people we love
are constructed into us,
bone on top of bone.

they are always in us,
like a quiet garden
or the moon's reflection.

the most difficult thing
for the most sensitive among us
is learning how to keep the light aflame
steadfastly, harmoniously, tenderly.

one way is staring into your
still and luminous sleeping faces.

this is my obligation
and the stunning privilege of life,
both beautiful and terrifying.

i know you are made of stars

and that you carry eternity
inside the deepest corners of your being.

i know that love is the mystery
of our human experience,
but it has certainly been solved in you.

can we?

no one wants to have a meaningless life.

it is a miracle we are even here at all
and fully capable of making memories.

our inheritance should be a depth of tenderness,
with boundless sympathy and compassion for all.

the human heart is an ancient thing,
able to always pledge devotion
to the beautiful fidelity of feelings.

we should be celebrating the lives
of those who have dedicated themselves
to the pursuit of something benevolent,
like love, or the possibility of love.

we've made it this far.

we've lived this much.

can we survive more?

can we love harder?

can we take the unwritten words and speak them?

can we do the same with our hearts?

can we lift our gaze skyward to the birds
and see what it means to be at the mercy of the breeze?

can we recapture our dreams from earliest youth?

can we recover our moments of discovery

and the way we once looked at each other?

can we display elegance in an unforgiving time,
as the earth tears itself apart daily?

yes we can.

we can look at history as echoes of the future

and find the redemption in the soul weary.

we can look past the bewilderingly
warped vision of reality
that movies and tv and social media portray,
and the damage it has already done.

we can remain hopeful
before the tragic structure of our being.

we can look past the bestowing of prizes and honors,
the winning and competing,
and see that beneath these achievements,
is nothing but the agony and ecstasy
of the human spirit.

and in this human spirit,
there is something truly divine
heading to an unrecognized eternity.

we can shudder each day,
starting as the hours begin,
at the notion that every single person we love
will leave us at some point,
and some, sooner than later.

our staggering fragility
is untranslatable and unsayable.

we will have no choice but
to keep them all extremely close,
and this will be our genuine moment of warmth,
and our final performance together.

the search

the searching at sunset…

the slow movement
the head down
looking for that stone
looking for that shell
looking for that piece of wood.

what are we actually searching for?

maybe a small truth,
maybe some understanding,
maybe a connection to things,
maybe a story carved into silence,
maybe the nature of our capacity for hope,
maybe the struggles of being human
and the art of being ourselves,

or maybe just something that can save us,
at least for tonight.

where did they go wrong

they chase jobs and value them at all costs.

they live far from their families.

they move away from their friends.

they lock the doors of their apartments.

they close the elevator as people approach.

they hire nannies to walk their children to school.

they spread out into homes behind fences and lawns.

they commute alone in cars.

they walk with headphones on.

they gather, staring at their phones.

the unraveling of this harsh
and graceless time continues;
just witness the fact that
53 million american's viewed
vogue magazine's met gala livestream in 24 hours.

which reminds me:
never look at what's in the spotlight.

look for your own light
and let it shine through you
because divinity is only found
in your soul.

try not to follow the masses,

and remember,
in the midst of the crowd,
keep your solitude and sweetness,
cancel out the echoes of judgment,
and the useless opinions of others.

the noblest thing you can do
is be effortlessly kind.
but not just effortless;
it needs to be a profound kindness

to everything that exists.

when the first bird of morning begins singing,
remember there is no separation
between you and the birdsong.

keep sensitivity and deep attention.

between the virtues of truth and meaning,
between knowing and thinking,
we can feel more deeply and more widely.

and if it comes to pass,
let your heart break open
and let life live in the two halves.

let both halves sit in silence
staring at each other,
balancing on the edge,
with the glimmering of sweet recognition
that each half is still bound as one.

54 bones in my hands

i still remember that night when the sea
was colored by the setting sun
and only an hour of daylight remained.

ours is a love undiminished,
radiating the larger truth
about our human hearts.

these are the most important
moments of our lives.

we embraced as the moonlight began
to feed us
and shade us
and gave us a place to rest.

i breathed your exhale
and stayed lost in your arms,
lost to your eyes.

remaining together
with the remembrance
that there are 54 bones in my hands,
and i held you with all of them.

true artists

talent and quality usually go ignored in this life,
and when and if they ever get some belated recognition,
even that is through happenstance.

true artists really don't want to be recognized.

they actually want to be removed from it all
and rise above the hollow desire for status.

it is never about popularity.

embrace great aloneness and aliveness.

look for the public benches to sit on;
they are your invitations,
the touchstones,
the anchors,
the reflections of our apertures.

inspire the ordinary,
the invisible,
and the forgotten,
all with a sense of majesty.

keep the fearlessness of youth
and the splendidness of affection.

stay quiet,
stay anonymous,
stay incomplete,
stay imperfect,
stay like my 10-year-old
daughter emma,
who constantly misjudges
how much space she has

on a line to write what she intends,
resulting in smaller and smaller,
tightly squeezed letters.

as she approaches the edge of the page,
somehow she gets all the words on the line,
and if she can't, she puts in under the next line.

it is quite beautiful.

i know the things i care for will continue
among gentle breaths during these
final chapters of life,
and with the revelatory
heartbreak of farewell,
because of you

i will leave this world, at last,
very serene and very still.

in the end

ever since i was about 13 years old,
i have often cried at unexplained moments
and at late hours of night.

i used to wish for night
to hide the beginning of my tears.

i guess it's a certain combination
of the day's burning and the night's dream,
of my parents and my brother,
and now my daughters.

when it becomes silent,
and i have only a small piece
of my mind left,

i will know that
to reach the stunning sunlight
of the following morning,
with you all around me,
is the only victory
worth raising your hands for.

forget the "great things"

it should not be in the presence
of so-called great things
that we feel the closeness of the divine,
but in the small everyday experiences
that bring us the realization
that all is found in our sensitivity.

we are programmed to expect happiness
from certain circumstances,
which will ensure certain disappointment
if not attained.

we continually inherit this
through the evening news and hollywood movies.

we are taught what is beautiful,
trained to see and feel,
and this is an absolute mistake.

life should be consumed with hope
and a restless yearning to refuse cynicism and sarcasm.
this alone will be among the greatest
accomplishments we can achieve.

face your life with equanimity, tenderness, and patience.

poetry is everywhere, all around our hearts, at all times,
and accessible to each and every one of us.

much like the tiny flowers reaching for the sun
during the season of beginnings.

the promise is always in the springtime air
as the birds gather to sing their songs.

i understand this now.

to the passing eye, it may seem unremarkable,
but i also know that the day fades
not into darkness, but into the generous sunsets
that shine a light
on the singular resilience of our benevolence
as we embrace the unknown and the unknowable
with unflinching miraculousness.

a stone to throw

i heard the slow, determined breathing
and how it rose and fell,
and then all was still.

and i was left with
just a voice inside
and a stone to throw,
but i had some music,
and music is always made in the past,
and it is the memory of who we are.

so with this, as the hours pass,
i will glimpse the unseen
and see beyond the horizons in front of me.

and everything will be different now,
the conversations i have,
the thoughts i reflect on,
the changes in the natural light and shadows,
the different breezes of the wind,
and the closeness of the moon and the stars.

birth

we are all born
looking for comforting eyes.

and where do we find
this immense capacity for love?

the love will always be found at home,
though i will continue to search
for my place under the sun and in the shade.

my life is reflowered as i blink slowly,
before i catch a little eternity
in a small room, in the city of new york.

i will stay right here and rejoice
in the glory of poetry and truth,
in the treasure of humility,
the grace of emotion,
the tranquil garden,
and of course,
this golden, undeniable solitude
that we share together and apart,
which endlessly enriches our story.

spread out before us

lying on the bed
in that unusual hotel room,
watching the lights of passing cars
sweep across the ceiling.

i thought of you
and how we walked side by side
through the ending of a century
and the birth of another.

with life breathlessly
spread out before us,
we have only this time,
which waits to be filled
by you and me.

my job

i'm trying to get these words down
because i know somewhere
someone is watching,
and one day my luck will turn around
or perhaps it won't and that will be ok too.

only they know when it will happen.

and either way,
it will be my simple victory,
and i will celebrate
like a celebration of your first love
and how that haunts you forever.

your eyes

my eyes seek your eyes,
where the progression of seasons
cross the tides of time.

though it is life,
it is at once
a fragile occasion
and a contribution to beauty,

beauty that stands out in relief
among unspoken, unheard sorrow.

the ache often turns
into numb despair
because of the short distance
to your heart
from the outside world,
and because you unshaded the sun
while wrapping my hands in flowers.

it is this trace of humanity and of nature
that will create our morning song of tears,
lamenting the coming of day when lovers must part.

brushed with hope
in a moment's blend of promise,
my dream reveals its purpose,

and your love will remain
as real as the poet's promise.

alone on a beach

the sky hung low and thick over the sand.

the sea stretched away with its drowsiness.

the sounds of night shivered in me.

i thought of you,
and i thought of the living in our life,
and it was as it should be.

i didn't have a single sad thought.

thank you.

making love

making love
under the brave sun in august.

making love
as the blue tv light surrounds all 4 walls.

making love
beneath a photograph of flowers.

making love
in small rooms while the moonlight filters through.

making love
in the middle of the day,
in the middle of the week,
when everyone else is getting yelled at by the boss.

you poor fools.

you have no idea what you're missing.

the cemetery

as the day moved on,
i passed the local cemetery
and paid a visit.

i walked across
the patches of frozen grass
as the morning light bounced
from headstone to headstone.

some were brand new;
others were broken and missing parts.

it reminded me for some reason
of pablo neruda and how he sat in his home
surrounded by those old wooden figureheads
from the old ships of spain.

it was a blue morning,
and i eventually returned to my writing,
which, as you probably know by now,
occurs in a small room in a building
off a rundown street
where i spend hours
holding hands with life and literature
by making small books
that you can stick in your back pocket
and sit on them when you feel like it.

my last words
for emma and mia

these last words are for you.

i'll always be watching.

the wind will be my voice,
and i hope the sound soothes you to sleep.

my love for you was always
timeless and tender and graceful.

i hope you notice this flower blooming;
it's the last one i planted for you at the house.

how do i explain the inexplicable,
or at least provide you a glimmer of hope?

devastating and vanquishing,
like the unpredictability of life.

i will miss you every day.

wishes come true sometimes, in unexpected ways.

hang in there, my loves;
i'm still here.
just look for the signs.

naked

the radio plays
in the room next door,
and she wants to be with you
just because she wants to.

and everything comes down
to this moment,
this bed,
this bottle of wine,
this song,

and this light
radiantly slipping through the curtains,
bouncing off your face onto mine.

holding on

unflinching through these moments,
we keep a poetic tenderness for each other,
holding on to a passion for possibility
and the promise of simply being alive.

we do not worship success
and the deadening pressure for productivity
at the cost of our freedom.

we know that our greatest unspoken truth
is simply watching the sun set in early evening,
and listening to the morning ocean.

it is the benediction of having enough.

it is the momentum of our lives,
a helping hand extended,
a smile from an elderly woman walking past,
a cardinal fluttering on the branch,
and the laughter of children from the nearby park.

it will also be something nameless
but entirely reachable,
like the repeated refrains of nature.

take them all in with genuine reflection
and the most elusiveness of love
will be yours alone,
day and night,
between sleep and wakefulness.

the books and the boy

i sit down tonight to write,
and i am surrounded
by bookshelves upon bookshelves.

all my favorites are here with me,
the great ones, waiting patiently

from
neruda to rimbaud,
hemingway to miller,
bukowski to kerouac,
fante to celine,
whitman to steinbeck,
tolstoy to kafka,
fitzgerald to joyce.

they get me through most days.

just seeing their names in the leather bindings
and glancing at the titles of their work:

"20 loves poems and a song of despair"
"illuminations"
"the sun also rises"
"stand still like the hummingbird"
"betting on the muse"
"ask the dust"
"journey to the end of the night"
"leaves of grass"
"the winter of our discontent"
"notes from the underground"
"tender is the night"
"war and peace"
"letter to his father"
"the sound and the fury"

"a portrait of an artist as a young man."

just the titles alone
are enough to make me weep.

that and the boy across the street
with the bouncing ball.

every day at the same time,
i hear a ball bouncing outside my window.

at first,
it was a little distracting,
but as i looked out
through the wooden blinds,
i saw a boy, about 7 years old,
bouncing a blue ball against his garage door.

he appeared happy and seemingly content.
he was alone.

he would bounce the ball off the garage door
and try to have it bounce back
within the square cement blocks in front of him,
and he would keep at it until it hit
his imaginary box every time.

there was something about that little guy
that made me want to keep writing.

perhaps it was his perseverance,
or perhaps it was the fact
that he had on 2 different sneakers,
one blue, one white.

whatever it was, i thank him,
the little one outside

and the great ones inside.

i want to thank them both
for the moments we spent together,
at this appointed time and place.

with great wonder,
we question where we are
and where we wish to go.

it is something deeply personal
yet universally profound,
echoing the togetherness of childhood
and the true attentiveness of being present
with full generosity toward humanity.

still in love

majestically,
with more human dignity than ever,
i see the joy on your face,
your contented smile,
and your unwavering words
as we stand together at the edge of time,
where our particular portion of eternity begins.

i cherish this warmth, aglow with hope.

we return to a home,
filled with books
and paintings and photographs,
and our children's boundless love.

every night before we turn off the lights,
we hold hands and are quiet together.

this is our small but enduring reminder
that our last thoughts of the day are of each other.

and the best part
is i will wake tomorrow
under the softness of the sky
and write these words
while i'm still in love.

question

i pass you on the sidewalk.

i sit across from you in the restaurant.

i glimpse you from your lighted window,
and i lock eyes with you briefly
as the city's dislocations appear and disappear.

but will i find you again after you fade from sight?

will our destinies become intertwined?

will spring's symphony of songbirds sing for us?

will we give ourselves over to joy as the hours unfold?

will we be granted a story of survival?

and will we come together,
learning warmth in each other's hands
as we walk past the shadows flickering
from the washed-out streetlights of new york?

the morning light

i have cried more than the first thousand men
you'll pass on the street,
but they will never know the secret
nor have the pleasure of seeing your face
in the 1/2 light of early morning.

even your words obliterate any sense of loss
that attached at this early hour.

you were the one.

and i will continue
to unsparingly bleed these words for you,
as the heartbreakingness of everything
dissolves sweetly with the remembrance of you.

an old's man life

i waited for answers in those rooms
those overpriced, undersized new york rooms,

where i spent so many nights
counting the holes in the
plaster-filled walls from the
now removed picture hooks.

i thought of the first photograph
i hung there, in-between the peeling paint,
and how it always kept me company.

i feel i may have weakened a bit
as i find myself learning to fly
while i'm falling.

most of us know how to be young
but never quite figure out
how to grow old,
especially with aloneness
being so much a part
of an old man's life.

but when i reach that point
and am burdened with
a loss for words,
a flash of despair,
a temporary collapse,
i will think of you
and how that one night i watched
as moonlight reflected through the soft air
and everything you were to me was illuminated
with the rapture of this undeniable,
boundless love.

1st day of work

looking past the unhappy faces,
i stare at the birthing of the morning sun
making its way over the east river;
something all the unhappy faces
don't seem to notice.

when i arrive at my awaited destination,
i pause and go to the restroom,
straighten my tie,
button my suit jacket,
fold the paper in two,
replay the song,
and tilt my head slightly upward
in order to stop the tears
from making their way down my face
at this early hour of day.

most work days are a ritual for many,
but the only ritual for me
will be the sacred one of ensuring
that my two daughters are safe
in their beds each night.

splendid isolation

our spirits unite
and the exuberant,
splendid isolation
that follows make
the views grow longer
and the promises grander.

the sun begins to sleep,
the city night emerges,
the traffic lightens,
the sounds grow quieter,
and the breeze rises elegantly
to swallow our souls.

to exist

the struggle to exist,
to not disappear in these moments,
to hang on to the urgent need for hope.

leave me alone so i can try to live quietly.

i am aware that it's almost
incomprehensibly miraculous
to have been granted any time at all,
to be here, uniquely human and sacred.

i will keep a remembrance for these fortunate hours.

i will not be careless and forget.

i will find the importance of my solitude.

i will howl at the majestic brevity of life,
both delicate and fleeting.

i will let the silence arrive
when i wrap my arms around those i love.

i know that moments are fleeting
but always the most beautiful.

i know the quality of our attention
shapes the quality of our lives.

i am trying now
to catch a small glimpse of heaven,
breathing into the unselfing of nature,
because i know it will be the waiting
for the flash of your smile

and the sound of your laughter
that will carry me through the centuries.

the ancient clouds

you made it possible
to navigate the stars at night,
and because of this,
all i can do is count the eternal minutes
until your splendid return.

i will remain present
in the great days of our love,
once delicate and unadorned,
and now unchanging on the edge of time.

the ancient clouds
testifying still that all is ok.

and thankfully,
i am left with the remembrance
of the quiet perfection
of waking up together.

if

if i die tonight,
at least i die yours.

ignore it all

we have allowed
the news,
the movies,
the fashion industry,
social media,
and the entire entertainment industry
to manipulate and destroy us
through the worshiping displays of
the show of wealth
the symbols of luxury
the ruling class
the temples of finance
the status obsessed
the dictates of how you look
the youth obsessed
the money making
the branding with labels
the shiny cars
the gleaming yachts
the sparkling jewelry
the enormous houses
the ambitious climbing
the corporate retreats
and on and on and on

all symptoms of our
desperate bid for society's esteem.

this kind of life will never win,
but it doesn't go away either

much like evil and madness.

what do we do then?

first, ignore it all.

then, forget judgement and go with uncertainty.

forget being right and go with understanding.

you don't have to follow
the edicts of modern life
and fill it with busyness and productivity.

our time is finite,
and we have no control
over how it will unfold
or when it will run out.

imagine you have only a year left,
what would you do?

imagine you have only a day left,
what would you do?

imagine you have only an hour left,
what would you do?

go with a little silence,
say less because they are always talking.

keep the fullness of life
and the vibrancy of love.

keep an uncommon sensitivity
to all living things.

pay attention to every moment,
and that is what your life will be.

your stories will shape who you become.

sharing the life of your heart
will enrich you beyond measure.

and know that love is all you have left,
and that life is our greatest work of art.

1,000 dreams

the heat of the sun
leaves us to sing our nightly songs.

and to think there are stars
100 times more massive than our sun.

but we two,
upon this earth,
lie in stillness,
with 1,000 dreams overflowing.

part of me withdraws weeping
after placing my eyes on you.

your hair falls about my face,
and i breathe in your breath
hoping i can endure
another night with you alone
as i surrender at midnight
to the deep calm of your heart.

i am able to see my children
reflected in your eyes.

the wakeful moon brings us honesty
but also lamenting
because dawn is the enemy of our time.

i wonder if we will be defeated
by the weight of our emotions.

but we will rise together
pushing melancholy off the pillow
as we untangle and then interweave
our exuberant life and love.

the awareness

i am humbled daily by the awareness
that among the trees and under the stars
is the only place one needs to go
to live peacefully,
and to affirm the resilience of life
and its worthiness.

let's not forget that
whales remember,
elephants grieve,
and all living things
tremble in the face of death.

know how to fill the in-between moments
with great gentleness.

have the ability to keep faith in uncertain things.

let the heart be stretched wide with awe.

keep a capacity for finding the reverence of now.

stay heartbroken but stay forgiving.

it's ok to be disrupted, and to be less productive.

gather yourself through love and loss.

embrace all emotions
and make something beautiful out of it.

go with the grace of surrender
and the resting into life.

wrap your arms around the glorious imperfections

that make us human,
and you will be granted a sincerity of spirit.

make one last grasp at light amidst the darkness.

gaze past the horizon
and straight into the radiance of love,
which you will find weeping with elation.

and watch this unfold
as if you're watching
the love of your life
sleep soundly into the gentle morning.

worthy of old age

look past work,
with its dread and distractions,
and instead look for the stories of vanished ages.

let's talk
about the sorrows we pour out.

let's return
to the quiet place inside ourselves.

let's wander
through the streets,
across cities and centuries.

let's discover
things we might have missed
had we not been paying attention.

let's walk
without destinations.

let's travel
through the relentlessness of time.

let's follow
the sound of church bells,
the clouds above,
and the breezes through the trees.

let's drift
across cobblestone squares,
through cemeteries,
across bridges,
along the rivers,
at the foot of mountains,

and under the afternoon sun.

let's stop to rest,
and anticipate the light
and warmth of the coming dawn.

tell me what you're thinking about
and what worries you.

tell me about the voices

you're desperate to hear.

we are of our own time,
living through this unusual era
in human history.

as this life continues
wearing down and falling apart,
let's pause with calm acceptance
and no anguishing anxiety.

let's welcome this spectacular love,
unexpected in common hours,
which allows our **disbelief to be suspended**
as we become worthy of old age.

the magical hand

you are the shimmering reminder
that any two people
can cross each other's path
at any given moment.

we weave the pattern of our destiny,
threading together
memories and remembrances
that remain in yesterday's shadow
and today's echo.

love is simply the magical hand
of our human experience,
and we will hold them
together now
and forever more.

father and son

driving
but looking right
to see a father walking
with his son along the sidewalk.

this moment catches me in my throat.

the song on the radio
is the same song that was on
when my brother called me to tell me
that our dad had just died.

as all the wonder and sorrow
rushes through the cracks of everyday life,
i am reminded of the bittersweet beauty
of this deeply human rite of passage.

i know we all exist
in magnificent, fragile bodies,
joyful and vulnerable all at once.

i will return home now and sleep.

and i will wake tomorrow
fully aware that each morning
we renew ourselves again,
and i will keep trying
to love more and live more.

the bird

i sit in the backyard among all this nature,
and i imagine the bird flying back to her nest
to fold her wings in tranquility.

it reminds me that the openness
of the heart's tenderness
is one of life's tremendous privileges.

my lungs have been given a gasp
on this blue morning as i stay quietly present.

i know that wonder is the act of remembering,
and i am thinking of all the people i love
and how they remind me of trees,
human trees if you will,
relentlessly reaching for the light of day.

in this beautiful old place,
my faithfulness to you will remain immutable,
and i will allow things to unfold
with a certain romance,
a little mystery
wrapped in eloquent simplicity.

i know this will
eventually fade into shadows,
but we will still have
our stolen moments at nightfall
and our story of surrendering to love
with plenty of hours to go
before we part
with our fragile aliveness.

win and lose

the victory of love and its rejuvenation
is in the braveness and truth
with which we live, uniting two people
for the time it keeps them together,

before having to let go at some point,
with equal braveness and truth.

my sorrow is complete

i will remain a family man,
even though she never really loved me.

i will remain an adoring father,
even though i miss them half the time.

families are displaced.

loved ones are gone.

my sorrow is complete,
and that is the saddest thought of all.

how will i live now when life is nearly over?

where do i end and the rest of life begin?

the big losses will have no name.

you may even find the impossibility
of articulating exactly what the pain consists of
as you feel the irrepressible lump in your throat,
but the substance of humanity will require you
to rebuild life and live more authentically.

despair and rejoice that your greatest loves
exist only for a time before saying goodbye.

life will most definitely
not unravel the way you want it to,
though you can remain intent
on holding this all so gently,
despite the injuries to your heart.

don't long for an unlived life.

there will be the unfair promise of loss
and the anguishing romance of winter.

as it nears,
my eyes will close,
and with all the prayers
my hands can make,
i will hopefully wake up
to put forth a small smile

and offer a little wave
to the people i love.

our planet will continue to tilt,
letting the sun set this evening,
and so too will our profound intimacy.

and with each modest breath,
i will love you still
with my whole broken heart.

what is success?

the resting into life will require
you to disregard the endless longing
to feel seen and valued,
and then you can live your life
without any self-doubt.

success always comes from within.

what matters is how you spend the hours
and minutes and seconds of life
when you're lucky enough
to even be here spending them at all.

you need to be honest in your expressions,
especially with your inner truths.

you can be normal
and extraordinary at the same time,
as long as you tend to your own heart rightly.

in your inner quiet,
the lines of poetry
will still sound sweetly
because our togetherness
will keep our love delicate at all times.

enoughness

together, in harmony,
under a pleasant sun.

it is the weight of living
marked by the wonder of possibility.

the feeling of enoughness
that makes our lives
worthy of having been lived.

i am still searching,
still wandering,
still fiercely celebrating the sunset
and our songs of love.

i see my daughters running
through the summer grass,
with birds overhead
and breezes through the trees.

and i hope they understand someday,
as i whisper to myself:

> *"you can see me best
> when you close your eyes."*

before death

the moment we experience before death
as we grasp for survival,
will be the last cries of our spirit.

our hearts and souls will long to experience
a vision of the thing we most want to see again.

and that, for me,
will always be
my daughters, emma and mia.

poetry

from youth to old age,
i have discovered that
poetry creates kindness.

i try to write about things
that hold their own history.

my fingers bleed as i write these words.

i weep still for every verse written.

nothing is unspeakable.

i still imagine the possibility of a final word.

and with this dedication,
nothing untrue will ever find its way
into my heart or onto these pages.

the story

as i walk,
the street lamps cast a soft glow on the trees,
and i am fully aware of this particular moment.

i let the music enter and magnify this time,
anchoring me in the stream of life.

carrying this story, an untold story,
and the forgotten way of seeing one another
and remembering there is always you.

i know so few win, so many lose,
but life should never be a competition.

life is about the music
and the persistence of hope,
not occurring to us, but through us,
intimately,
with a glance,
a nod of the head,
a slight smile,
even a shrug,
or a sigh.

every embrace we make inches us closer to the truth.

and as i prepare my farewell,
i cherish all of it now because of you alone.

fragments

trying hard not to stop the wakefulness of life
in order to avoid feeling all the pain.

we live in a world
that continually fragments
and fractures us.

i have always been aware of this,
delicately and completely

i'm not suppressing my sensitivities,
and i'm not teaching my children
to suppress theirs.

we will allow love to absorb us.

if you let yourself see beauty,
then you will also see ugliness.

if you open yourself to happiness,
then you will also open yourself to sorrow.

there is no other way.

be unafraid to feel,
stay with an emotional life;
it is the only things that makes a difference,
where every word is weighed,
and it brings nothing but
full, transcendent poetic resonance
in between the weeping that fills up your eyes.

our children

the fixtures of childhood,
with our own children
wrapped with warm hands,
reminds us that the full life
is the sunrise of awe
and the serenade of becoming.

like driving to the bay
to see the sunset,
searching and finding
those smooth stones,
those extraordinary shells
before the eternal sea
and among the unbounded clouds.

these moments of discovery
are our way of looking
for a glimpse of truth,
for particles of humanity
that will illuminate
the interconnectedness
of everything we see and feel.

opening ourselves
to the capacity for being moved
as opposed to acquiring, competing,
producing, and climbing.

even if momentarily,
it is still wonderment,
and still an epiphany among our splendid
and splendidly captured moments.

against all the staggering odds,
we still wake each morning

and get to experience the astonishment
of this sky, these trees, this ocean,
and, of course,
these loves that we live for.

a foreboding

yours was a soul-splitting death.

the palpitations remain in my chest,
my nerve endings are inflamed,
my old wounds are throbbing.

walking along ancient paths,
your presence was always
my most needed consolation.

my eyes, lensed now
on the unspoken
and the withheld,
my lifetime of experience.

exuding love as naturally
as summer turns to autumn,
autumn to winter,
winter to spring,
and back to summer.

i look for these repeated refrains of nature
and take them all in as intimately as possible.

closing my eyes and willing my way
back to sleep.

each word needs to be spoken with gentleness now,
and with the promise of completeness.

when the sun slips below the horizon,
its light will be refracted on us,
on our frailties,
on our closeness,
all at the heart of a fulfilling life.

this is where we lived and loved.

this is our peerless portrait.

i ask these disquieting questions
to no one in particular:

is death like birth?
is sorrow like joy?

is an ending like a beginning?

you are a celebration of our memories
and all that remains undone.

loving you brings nothing but
a delightful exhaustion
into an exhale,
with shared memories
and the meaning
of you to me.

i am suffering and recovering.

the moment i lost you
is the moment the weight of melancholy
and the totality of desolation was complete.

through this anguish,
i will still grasp for love
and all that comes with it.

my hope now will be,
if my soul is strong enough,
to see your face again.

the human experience
[september 12, 2023]

diagnosis.
prognosis.

the most heartbreaking,
most humbling,
most harrowing news.

how will i continue
to write these words for you
in this time of trauma?

where are the silent sounds of yesterday?

can i have a quiet moment of reflection
to find what's human and magical still?

i climb into bed next to my 8-year-old daughter
and hear the first teardrop hit the pillow.

both of us deeply sensitive
and always struggling with
the turbulences of our human hearts.

i place my hand on her warm sleeping back,
and the weeping begins.

this captures some of the enormity of my love,
and all of humanity radiates as a testament
to the true splendor of being human,
the astonishing capacity for love,
and the boundless richness that exists between us.

i will wake tomorrow
and walk under the sun,

touch a patch of earth,
and whisper a prayer to us all.

self-worth

don't you see that the ones mocking your fragility,
or any tenderness for that matter,
are the same ones
who deny any vulnerability?

they don't realize that their net worth
has nothing to do with their self-worth.

don't be like them.

don't hide your feelings
beneath the numbers in your bank book,
your big house,
your nice car,
or your bright children.

living in our competitive
and consumerist society
makes everyone status conscious,
so the discontented ones buy more stuff,
and the system hums along nicely,
thriving on bad feelings,
and keeping most grasping
ever upward with no end in sight.

at work we are tracked and ranked
and made to feel it could all be pulled out
from under us at any moment.

they want this.
it's the insecurity
that results from the expectation
and the deprivation of your being.

no one is superior to you.

when they tell you they are not something,
that is precisely who they are.

don't bend under the weight they give you.

don't let your heart break.

keep friends in low places if you have to,

those are the ones
who will stay with you when needed.

and we all need care throughout our lives,
and true sentiments; how people actually feel.

embrace the painful privilege of knowing
the human search for meaning.

writing a poem.

raising a child.

composing a love letter.

gathering flowers.

putting the seeds gently into the ground.

making it easier for us to breathe.

the living moment.

the passing minute.

the pulse of your heart.

the infinite inside you.

it is your way of moving through this life,
experiencing others with truth and concern
rather than desperation and distress.

hold on to this place of reverence and responsibility.

keep your determination for gratefulness and hope
and your timeless testament to the fullness of feeling
at being touched by the last rays of the departing sun,
or in the fading autumn light,
when life has begun to feel livable again,
even beautiful.

although we are present in this fragile place,
we can still recognize the cathedral of chance
for what it means to be part of this world
and the ongoing mystery of who we are

and the majesty of those we love.

and with this,
we can think more deeply,
feel more fully,
dream more boldly,
and live more wholeheartedly.

all we need to remember is
the brevity and beauty of this
and that it may never come again.

this i know to be the truth

is there anything better than
approaching a door at the end of a day
knowing someone on the other side
is waiting for the sound of your footsteps?

and then to go to bed, sleepless,
next to that same person,
with their eyes, ears, nose, arms, feet, and ankles
all intertwined with yours.

this is the birthplace of love.

hold this integrity of being awake to life,
which also means being awake to mortality.

but don't try to solve the mysteries;
revel in them.

when you know what is enough,
you will feel joy.

you will hold
the absolute commitment for affection
to your fellow human beings,
and you will know,
you will always know,
that one final embrace
is your shield of personal love
for your participation in this life.

silence is the experience of time passing

i need more silence.

i need these moments of quiet.

the hush at the end of music,
the pause in a close conversation,
the muted moment when we climb into bed,
savoring the living in us
and, above all,
the gratitude for each other,
with moments of reflection and illumination.

this is the **very thing**,
with emotions emerging,
inspiration flowing,
desires pulsing,
and the **reverence for life**
outpouring everything good in us
from kindness to consideration to attention.

meaning

each of us is necessary

at this time,
in this place,
with irreplaceable intimacy.

we can't know everything;
we can't control everything;
and we can't predict everything.

but with the unfolding of time
and the passing of civilizations,
we awake to the here and now
to find the elemental truth
and the tenderest magic,
which is found
in every flower,
in every star,
in every moon,
in every child.

and the message in all
is that to be alive in this moment is enough.
it is always enough.

the music of our time

the harmony of the sun and the moon,
the ebb and flow of the tides,
the sunrise and the sunset,
the pulses and rhythms of nature,
our four beautiful seasons.

this is our hymn from ancient times
to the earliest days of our story;
it is the song of life,
and it is our intimate portrait
of profound hope.

disregard them

there is nothing money can't ruin,
the material way many try to fill up their lives.

forget the egoists,
who consider their talent self-earned
and their success self-made.

there will also never be corporate benevolence
or any sort of legislative nobility
as we spend our days
in the shadows of enormous companies
hungry for low-wage workers.

we've become inured to suffering,
absolving ourselves.

people just don't seem
to care enough about the welfare of others.

no amount of suffering will allow them to turn away.

then there's the beauty game,
controlled by the not so beautiful
who grab fortunes from it
and don't care who they hurt.

disregard the advertisers and marketers
trying to sell you things
by getting you to imagine
a better life for yourself.

what about relieving some of the suffering
or trying to improve the human condition?

how do we handle those who continue

to drain the sustenance of life
so that a very small percentage
of the population can live comfortably?

all you can do is stay sure-footed on your path,
both unplotted and untrodden by others
as you walk to the limitless horizon.

look up briefly with a soft, infinite yearning,
pausing to catch your breath

and turning to realize
that we were together the entire time.

our next moment will surely
not contain what this one lacks.

let's stay enchanted
with the interwoven life of nature
because your hands
look like starfish now
when they are holding mine.

and don't forget,
you were the first spark that struck,
catching fire and bursting
into pure flames
inside my heart.

my escape

i have escaped from the distractions.

i have been left alone to read
and recite poetry to the sky.

these words
that the unbroken solitude
has inspired in me
keep me with the living world,
and all these fragments of my life
remain with you.

what we did was love

on summer days we woke up,
had some homemade coffee,
read some poetry and some quotes.

went outside to the garden,
pulled some weeds
and some fresh fruit
and vegetables.

refilled the 3 bird feeders.

went for a bike ride along the water,
squinting the whole time in the sun.

had lunch.

drove to the sunset.

walked the edges of the beach,
picking shells and stones.

watched the sky change color
and the clouds move away.

retuned home for dinner,
opened a bottle of red wine.

read books
sitting across from each other
in the living room by the fire.

and then went to sleep.

what we did today was love.

when is the last time

the words you share in the middle of the night
may end up being the last ones spoken.

the embrace you give when parting;
you won't know if that's the final farewell.

the kiss shared in private,
not knowing if we will ever touch again.

your father's voice on the phone,
which you may never hear again.

ask yourself what you ache for.

what makes you shiver under a blue sky?

which memory will you not allow to be swept away?

behold the splendor
and elegy for a way of life
that only you know how to live
and that is filled with the art of substance.

presence

the poetry of existence,
the unfolding of our
wellspring of meaning,
and the breathtaking ways
we respond to the transience of everything.

with reality laid bare
and the self being most awake
to life's fragility,

we live with this unvarnished truth
about what it means to be alive,
because one day our eyes will no longer
look out on things we cherish.

by the grace of chance
we are here
to think,
to feel,
to reflect,
without any final answers
as the birds of summer sing to us.

we live
before a universe,
sometimes invisible
to the naked eye,
but we continue with
honorable and generous lives,
reflecting with luminous determination
to do better tomorrow than we did today.

unconquerable love

what i have is enough

it's always the little joys,
the things that are unpurchasable.

the sea that fills in the silence,
the shells that crack under foot,
the sunlight that refracts through the clouds,
the trees that stand with generosity,
and my daughters' wordless willingness
to care for our shared life and love.

without the brilliance of the day,
and the busyness and the hurry,
at night, i find a deeper quiet
among the magical sparkle
of the fireflies below
and the patient stars above.

i know that in the end,
as all light fades just above the treetops,
i will see the rising of the nearly full moon,
and i will bend my gaze to the last horizon
to look for you.

i beg you to stay,
at least until tomorrow,
to soothe my aching yearning for closeness.

love alone makes our tender,
transient lives worth living
and helps with these delicate
and fleeting moments.

this is my invitation

to rediscover life's priorities.

embrace the uncertainty of this all,
and never guard against the hurt.

stay open to doubt,
to being wrong,
to not knowing,
and to keeping silence,

which is not absence at all,
but the presence of everything
that allows us to remember
what we have forgotten,
because life will never be without reason.

as we catch a rare glimpse
of the words and books that change us,
neighborhoods we move into,
places we visit,
the ocean in the distance,
the night sky,
the enchanted sand under our feet,
the silver white moon…

and of course,
the solemn tenderness
and the delicate delight
of your unconquerable love.

beauty

i see these tiny flowers
and how they improbably grow
in the middle of inhospitable cement,
flourishing and colorful,
clinging to life,
weathered and battered.

the light is soft,
there is a breeze.

i don't want to speak much anymore,
but i want to write.

i want to remain comfortable in the discomfort.

i want to keep a reverent remembrance
for the irreversible past
and the incomprehensibility of the future.

i want to hold the pain and the beauty.

i want to find it in the unremarkable
and focus on the feel of the sand under my feet,
the look of the scattering clouds,
the taste of the day's ice cream,
this evening's sunset,
and in our small and simple moments.

and with this,
i know the grandness of human goodness
will be reflected
in the subtlest of touches
and in the briefest of words.

it is in the noticing
that we will find all the love.

fully human

stay courageous enough
and awake enough to
step into your own shadow
and embrace your imperfections,
because that's what makes you fully human.

it is the deepest part of you,
and it is the living moment
when you take it
from mere existence
to enveloping magic.

to-do list

breathe in the spring air,
feel the grass underfoot,
the tender afternoon light,
the visions of peace and consolation.

let the memories guide your path and your vision;
keep an eye always on the night sky
under which all is spread out with dreamlike elegance,
and the acceptance of the passage of time.

and like the passage of time,
the music's notes and silences
will be love's meaning and echoes
that will help us get through this night
and live well with the remaining time we have.

you and me

your hand forever is all i want.

can you hold me under the stars
and among the trees,
along with the bones and shells
bleached by the sun and sea?

let's find meaning
amid the uncertainty of being,
because to understand and be understood
is still one of life's greatest gifts.

i want to feel your warmth upon me,
to feel the entirety of who you are
and what you have lived with.

every memory and remembrance,
every love and every loss.

i want your magnified breathing
from your deepest place of reckoning
to your most significant place of wholeness.

i want the audacity of your heart
to guide the priority of our survival.

let's live together now with kindness,
the noble flame that keeps us alive.

we are present today, that is certain,
and every day with you
is a deep and enduring miracle.

let's live together now
with the understanding of our minds

and the celebration of our hearts
as we show each other
what it's like to be alive
as this sun and these shadows
shape the quality of our life.

each day i see your face and hands
colored by the sun,
and know it is only one thing,
unassailable love.

work

it's beginning to look
as if i'm actually going to have
to work for a living,
but i will remain apart from most,
except for that small, humble
noble percentage of the human race.

i will wrap my arms
around the belief that there will always be
a certain trueness to everything i see
as long as you're by my side.

with candles still burning,
the revelation of our truth together
and our enriching endeavor is now complete.

19-second tear drop

in the car alone
the song comes on
and i feel it all fully.

i look in the mirror
and i see the teardrop begin,
but it's a quiet one,
as it slowly makes its way
out of my left eye.

i count the seconds
as i watch it move down my cheek.

it takes 19 seconds to reach
the bottom of my face.

it was the slowest tear
i have ever experienced.

and with the gentle elegance of listening,
i could actually hear it moving
as my mind contemplated
the delicate harmonizing
of both grief and gladness.

love of life

in the raw moments following
the diagnosis averaging 2-5 years until death,
i was reawakened into a new cherishment of life,
although i have always had it.

nothing much changed to be honest.
i'm not despondent over the news,
and i haven't lost heart for this life
as i face these last moments.

what makes me disenchanted,
diminished, and a bit haunted
will be saying goodbye to my beautiful daughters.

they have been nothing less
than a benediction to me
and an awakening to this pure love of life
and the fragility we now inhabit.

i know now that it is possible
for children to guide us.

i look upon my past years
and smile, as no time was ever lost.

i never failed to value life,
always remaining grateful
with a full understanding
of how it all works.

a way of seeing differently,
more willing to find my own way,
and always knowing the true meaning of life
as the complete love of my parents, my brother,
and my daughters have allowed me

to take less materially secure paths in life
and always recount the enchantment of words
that will always stay with me.

i hope you find these words introspective,
without slipping into melancholy.
i am simply trying to give you subtle moments
of hope, romance, and a little warmth.

thank you for this love of life, which will continue.
some unusual things about me and maybe some advice

jealousy and envy are emotions i have never felt.

boredom i have never experienced.

i rarely turn on the tv.

i don't watch sports.

i don't go to strip clubs.

i don't watch adult films.

i will not wear clothing with brand names on them.

i don't like cars, especially expensive ones.

i will never define myself through the 9 to 5 hours.

i will always live at a slight acute angle to society.

i like to look at the books on my shelf
and know the pages are pressed close against each other.

i know that sometimes we don't make decisions,
we discover them.

i never got angry at someone who cheated on me. and there
have been a few. and if that's their choice, then it's their choice.
accept it truthfully and with compassion.
give immediate forgiveness.

i never got upset if excluded or not invited to something,
whether at work or in life. again, if that is their choice, accept it
with some mercy.

if someone ignores me or becomes difficult to contact or talk
to, look elsewhere. no desperation is ever needed.

being wrong and making mistakes are precious gifts,
so cure the addiction of always wanting to be right
and hiding errors.

i have always believed that all art should be free,
whether a painting or a book or a song.

there is a very simple truth to this life:
what and whom you love is your lens to everything.

i know the measure of a life
has to do with how much kindness
we can bring to humanity.

i believe deeply in bearing witness
to all facets of the human experience.

people rarely say what they truly believe,
and you don't have to believe what they say.

i remember the subtle truths in simple terms.

i still see the faces and hands
of everyone i have ever loved.

i believe in love's promise of the heart
and how this remains the silent witness
to our countless human heartaches.

to make works of art and bring some truth,
one has to feel fully the love of life.

let creativity drown out the fear and the noise.

have conversations of true listening,
with no set agenda or goal on what to reply.

don't have expectations on what time covers,
or what it has to result in,
or what it has to produce.

let the stillness of your soul
be the glint of romance you need
in these sometimes cruel and confusing times.

remember the sun always inches closer
to the horizon and winds down for the day
with a gentle and poetic ballad of love.

the self who feels most tenderly
will do so with such serenity
that the definition of love

will give a voice to the unsayable.

our breathtaking benevolence will bring
life-giving and life-saving magic
for another way of seeing.

this raw and rapturous way of being
will be woven into the fabric of our experience,

with closeness and distance,
intimacy and estrangement,
separation and exposure.

as we ask:

do we withdraw from it all or try to change it?

and this question's fragility
will radiate with assurance
that the world will continue,
and that we are part of something magnificent
that anchors us all to eternity.

impermanence and presence

have gratefulness and appreciation
for the sheer wonder of being alive.

do not allow the immediacies of everyday life
and the constant stress make you miss these moments.

keep always a generosity of character
as there is pure beauty that springs
from our inevitable impermanence.

awash with news and information
but vacant of wisdom and integrity,
how do we make our moments matter?

as our portrait of life unfolds,
we can first make the staggering revelation
that it is a great miracle to be alive together
and to have the ability to transfer tenderness
from any sorrowing of heartbreak.

presence is our essential form of love,
so stay present and stay quietly contemplative.

the very act of writing or painting
or composing or singing
or just walking while holding hands,
is a hopeful act often marked by struggle
and untouched by recognition,
but that is more than ok,
because with art
comes a touch of eternity.

our search and discovery of our true light
unfolds amid unseen and unsure things
as does the tranquility over how

to really love one another.

because how we spend
our waking moments,
our minutes, our hours, our days,
is precisely how we live our lives.

the wellspring of my heart

the wellspring of my heart
is waiting without expecting
anything to happen.

just waiting, because the only thing to do
is surrender and embrace
the magical mystery of loving this one
and not the other.

what am i going to do

mia comes into my room and says:

> *"hey, dad,*
> *you are like my mom and my dad*
> *wrapped up in one person.*
> *i love you so much.*
> *what am i going to do when you die?"*

she then asks for my t-shirt
and to spray some cologne on it
so she can wear it to bed
smelling and thinking of me.

mia did the same thing
with her grandfather's shirts
after he died.

the ennobling effects of this absolute wonder
allows me to surrender to the gentle gift
of this pure heart.

it has taught me to care more
about virtue than success,
enjoy greatly,
be delicately honest,
keep unflinching tenderness,
stay imperfect,
live with mystery,
embrace uncertainty,
go with a little solitude,
have the fortitude to know myself,
and engage in a life
of creativity and contemplation
while continuing to always keep
planting the seeds of compassion.

mercy

remember

what they don't like in you is missing in them.

they are always pushing, inching, needling,
cheating for some insignificant advantage
that means nothing.

let them have it.

give them their small victories.

like the car that cuts in front of you;
they need it because they have nothing else.

the lesson they will never learn
is the less you need, the better you will feel.

they don't know moments of great stillness.
they don't understand the bittersweetness of life.
they don't embrace the fidelity of feelings.
they don't have attentiveness for other human beings.
they don't realize there is nothing to prove.
they don't see the long golden sunlight of late afternoons.
they don't distance themselves from the inessential things.
they don't know about the timeless lens of ancient wisdom.

we continue, though, knowing

there are divine things in the midst of chaos,

there is boldness in being tender,

there is eloquence in knowing time is running out.

and when the end comes,
i wish them all nothing but mercy.

heartbreak

heartbreak is the emblem of care
and the very essence of being human.

it is inescapable love,
and it's the realization of our humanity.

gratitude

be the author of your life.

define your worth on your terms
and what a successful life
looks like to you only,
not to anyone else.

remember that the best way
to get approval and applause
is to have the certitude
not to need it at all.

this is true for just
about everything in life.

pay loving attention
to noticing and noting
everything around you,
despite the fact
that we can count on
so few people.

keep and nurture
the intelligence of emotions
and the heart's purpose.

it is difficult sometimes
to be a human being
full of understanding and gentleness,
but my predominant feeling
is one of gratitude.

gratitude for what
i have been given by others.

gratitude, too, that i have been able
to give something back.

i have had that specialness
between writers and readers,
which often quiets the mind
and quickens the spirit.

show up with integrity of intention,
and please, please, please,

don't realize what you have
when you are about to lose it,
and don't start to live
when you are about to die.

realize what is essential every day
and make time for it,
hold on to it desperately.

know the silence of waiting
as you wrap your arms around
the immutable concerns of love
and aging and the passing of time.

live without mask or pretension,
revealing the hidden intimacies of your life,
and you will never suffer a moment's
abatement of your spirit.

your love will outlast your losses,
and you will discern the honorable thing to do,
the loving thing to do,
as the correct shape of your heart
will be yours alone,
and the endless expanse of this
will continue, undiminished.

try

each of us is a living verse in this poem,
breaking from the crowd
and falling upon us like a benediction.

darkness falls early now,
so treasure the nobility and subtlety of life,
and recite this poetry and sing these songs.

make the season of change the season of rest,
and be grateful for the irreducible moonlight.

we are here, alive and well,
with our burning patience
and our symphony of feelings.

we are filled with the splendors and the sorrows
and the ephemeral and the eternal in us.

the years will pass in an eyeblink,
so we need to ask what is this life
and how does it live inside us?

the answer is simple:
we are the fateful decisions
we make every day,

and we will always remain a part
of this continuance,
holding on through the darkness
until the radiance returns.

the one

find the one who becomes more devoted
as the years go by;
that is the rarity and the revelation.

i only ever wanted a few,
a very few,
since a young age,
to accompany me on this walk of life.

i ask what are the daily mercies
we should never take for granted?

when you have the one,
you will have a life of destination.

along this arrow of time,
you will find that in the middle of the crowd,
you can have serenity.

in the midst of bewilderment,
you can have tranquility.

in the midst of tumult,
you can have harmony.

it's never the grand gestures
but the little things that add up over time.

it is these catalogue of moments that define love,
and it will be a breathtaking delicacy.

sleep

sleeping in a dreamless sleep
your hand always remains within reach
as we lie here like thoughtful searchers
of life's elegance.

i know that in one night,
we could dream back everything lost.

little by little
our kisses return
and race through the blue of night
into the gray of morning.

put both hands over your heart
and close your eyes.

beholden to none,
impassioned and immensely hopeful,
we can be a wondrous monument to being alive.

our declaration of love,
the highest human emotion,
is nothing more than an anticipation of eternity,
with remarkable patience and gratitude.

we have found something much larger
and more transcendent,
something beyond the sweetness of togetherness.

it is here where truth is unveiled,
questions are answered,
and flowers bloom in earnest.

we can feel awe in the air
as we fall back in love

and softly exist together now,
lifting our eyes to the same stars.

love

the work of love,
the rush of love,
the task of love,
the miracle of love.

this is our divine invitation,
our eloquent timelessness,
our serene grandeur,
our graceful gifts,
and our ancient places of reverence.

this human wonderment makes life bearable
and better understood because, in the end,
we lose everything that exists to us.

trying not to be overwhelmed
by the weight of these moments,
we can love more
because of the delicacy of it all.

and this is what we keep now
as i gently tuck the blanket
under the edges of your body
each night as you sleep.

the resilience of life

life is not easy at times,
and most people are drawn
to the easy way of living.
but the truth lies in surrendering
and never in the attempt to control.

every love and every loss
will shape the way we live
and provide us with timeless remembrances.

find the secret path and the divine unknown,
the impossibility of things
where our souls expand with prayerful dedication
to live more deliberately and authentically.

don't let criticism or jealousy sink you,
fiercely disregard the tide of your time,
and let the intimacy penetrate all you are.

hold your breath if you have to,
pause at midnight with fragments of memory,
and like children sleeping,
your peace and breathing will be
the resilience of life
and the endurance of love.

these flowers

these words,
this music,
and these flowers,
petals of compassion
like an outstretched hand
reaching for another,
urging the eyes to stay awake.

keep your consideration
because the most meaningful gifts
we have to offer are time and attention.

yes…
grief is what happens with time,
but joy will always linger in the end.

so reach for the shimmering instant of gladness,
because it's getting late and the moon is rising.

lyrics and words

when you can't find the words,
find the lyrics,
and the grace notes
will come after that.

let them radiate
an aching recognition
of what to conceal and what to reveal.

let them be
quietly revelatory
and gently gleaming,
telling your story
of woven remembrance and reflection.

try not to be overwhelmed by life,
knowing we can't bend
the universe to our will,
holding on to the
pristine moments of childhood,
and learning when to pause
so we can put a little space
between the here and there.

try to live
with uncommon authenticity
and move through life
with no loss of hope,
staying open to the
vast miracle of nature and ourselves
as we continue,
as sovereign souls,
with the full understanding now
of the complete definition of love.

emma and our unshadowed lives
[october 17, 2023] 10:03pm

emma comes out of the bedroom crying
and says:

> *"what am i going to do when you die, daddy?*
> *i love you so much.*
>
> *why did grandpa have to die so early?*
> *i wish i had more time with him."*

emma, here is my answer:

> *"we have to embrace the tenderness*
> *from these thoughts and emotions*
> *of all of our moments together.*
>
> *you and mia are my place in the sun*
> *until the end of my days.*
>
> *you are the most meaningful*
> *and sacred relationship in all of my life.*
>
> *yours is still the most abiding*
> *and beloved voice that whispers to me still.*
>
> *my love for you will be delivered*
> *with purity and warmth.*
>
> *everything will hold for us*
> *over the sweep of time.*
>
> *it's one of the greatest gifts*
> *of our life together.*
>
> *these poems, these prayers, these songs,*

*are for you always,
and they will remain,
which allows us to live unshadowed lives.*

blessings

in this exceedingly rare time
with nights and evenings of endless skies
and blazing sunsets unseen by most of us,
the attendant cry is heard
for a new way of loving
and a whole new way of perceiving.

the blessings are now counted
for what we have to fill:

the enchantment of darkness,

the poetry of solitude,

the eternity of tranquility,

the serenity of reticence,

and the celebration of the sky.

all a sense of earthly adoration,
captured and held tightly with both hands.

and because of these blessings,
maybe someday i'll heal
from all the things i don't talk about.

stars at night and our fragile hearts

if you confront your mortality,
you will have a chance to live more fully.

especially when so many people
anesthetize themselves by drinking
or shopping or numbing their way
out of themselves
when we actually just need
more endurance.

we must not ever live unexamined lives.

at the heart of human suffering
is a fear of the unknown,
of what can't be controlled.

we need to dismantle that artifice and cruelty.

we should be explorers and not followers.

we have to remember
it is always our dust and ashes
that give us our meaning.

the body will of course decay,
but our essence will endure,
to be present,
to love,
to write poetry,
to compose music,
to paint on canvas,
and all will add a little eternity to our everyday lives.

what we create can be profound and inextinguishable.

we should believe in expansiveness
and in the admiration for life.

we should live in harmony and placidity.

we should stay serene and sublime.

we should have a romantic view of human nature.

we should revisit good books and places,

paintings and people,
even a smile with a stranger.

let's listen again to that piece of music.

let's not be spiritually unsettled.

let's keep our eyes on 2 sacred things:
the stars at night and our fragile hearts.

the gentle touches are always found at home
because the people we built our life with
will no longer be here at some point.

let's appreciate the vulnerability
that comes with getting older.

understanding is one of the most
generous gifts we can give to one another.

let's end with reading
the secret map of our skin,
and this landscape of living
will be ours to celebrate
with our simple words,

because just the sound of your voice
is my greatest comfort of all.

until the rest of mine

emma and mia,
you are my world,
and you are the last in time.

i won't be around for the rest of your lives,
but i promise you both,
i will love you for the rest of mine.

live

i try to live in a way that allows me
to keep pursuing a life of meaning
through poetry and art.

trying to understand
what makes a human life purposeful.

perhaps it is the language of love,

those 3 words that bind us together,

the weightless breath that carries these words to you.

i bear witness to the vital substance of living
and the silent speaking of time
because, no matter what the ending,
the essence of us will always remain.

i miss you dad and thank you mom

i could not tell
whether my dad knew i was by his side,
but i heard that those close to death
retain their hearing long after
the other senses give out.

hopefully that's true,
and hopefully he knew he was not alone.

in the late sunset of tonight
and the early dawn of tomorrow,
the songs of silence
bring the absence of anguish,
and i have the answer now
to the question of whether
earth is the right place for love.

there will never be another such as you.

you were my life's moment of pure joy.

you were honorable and compassionate.

i saw how you treated other people,
and i saw how you handled being a physician
and a healer.

you didn't sit me down
and give me lectured advice;
you just lived a certain way,
and that was the best advice i could have gotten.

your love was ennobling and immensely delicate
but essential to who i am and what i have become.

authenticity is perhaps
the only real measure of success in this life
as we long for meaning, for truth, for love.

and you provided all of that for us.

you gave us the profound insight of truth,
generously offered through moments
of reflection and illumination
on the true fabric of love.

my face grows older now around sad eyes,
and i feel as if i have melted quietly
into the ocean of time,

but i will continue to honor you
with this blood of life
that drips from pen to paper.

i will do my best to live with
a sincerity of spirit
and the quiet grief requiring no words.

i will try to give some warmth to the world,
despite what the world has taken away.

and this warmth is found in you, mom.

i am immutably drawn to your light,
and your beauty alone
makes deliberate time for self-reflection,
which calms the disquietude of this haunted hour.

in the unspoken balance of
longing for presence and echoed absence,
the shattering luminosity of your heart
unburdens any self-pity or despair i may have,

and soothes me beyond the reach of words.

i look, and see, and understand
differently because of you.

you taught me that we are actually ok,
and it's not us, but the world that needs changing.

you built a family
around impenetrable strength,
where no one could hurt us.

and the closeness needed was always given.

your hovering heart is always visible to me.

mom, tell me a tender tale.
tell me something about the meaning of life.

you showed us how to gracefully

be fully and honestly human.

that it is in the significance of small gestures,
the universal experience of change,
and the precarious and unpredictable nature of life.

the restoration of lost truth

the togetherness and the separateness

the beautiful consciousness of being different

the blessedness of the stories that shape our lives,

and the enchanting glimpses in the enormity
of our indispensable heartbeats.

10 questions to ask

1) if you died today, what would you regret not doing?

2) can you be yourself and still fit in?

3) what talent are you not using?

4) where did you grow up?

5) where did you get your name from?

6) who is the love of your life?

7) what is your most cherished memory of childhood?

8) what is your favorite music, poem, and painting?

9) what is the brilliance and the horror of this world?

10) who is the person you will miss the most when they go away?

these bones are aching

these bones are aching a little now;
they seem to be getting weaker every day.
but my mind and heart are still burning at night
with the intimacy of personal remembrance.

i glimpse what no mirror can reflect.

i know the path of promise
and the richness that exists
because of the enormity
of your tender heart
and the astonishing capacity for your love.

it's the song of being wrapped
in uncompromising truthfulness.

the victory of this love
has been stirring and all eclipsing,
full of grace and fragility.

do we join humanity's
collective cry for mercy,
with its certitudes and platitudes,
or do we just lift our heads
and gaze at the unfathomable heavens
for the undiscovered beauty
that awaits us all?

maybe we can live more fully now,
approaching our time on this planet
with a certain relaxedness,
of knowing what to notice,
and how to live a good life,
filled with uncontainable gratitude.

the sun will set with devoted care,
vitality, and resiliency,
and our thoughts will be about
the choice to live now
with the ordinary wonder of days.

just us

4 degrees at the house

silence and snow

not a squirrel in the trees
not a bird on the feeders
no deer roaming the front
no rabbits bouncing by

just us.

and we know it's a fragile time for love,
especially since love remains
the enchanted enigma of our experience.

but this is how i wanted it today.

just us.

with the gentle elegance of certainty
and genuineness and generosity.

the unexpected gift of time was given to us,
and we have no concerns today.

i won't do any work around the house,
i promise, but of course,
i'll carry my heart for you.

we are made of stars

the fabric of being is our astonishment
as you can actually trace back
the atoms in our bodies
to some particular star
that died or exploded long ago.

the scientists have said that when stars die,
new elements are born, like calcium for our bones
and even oxygen for our breath.

we feel all of this because we are part of it all.

we have no choice but to live
with unflinching openheartedness
and really see the blueness of blue.

we can seek now the love that we need,

understanding that the mirrors
to ourselves depend on whom we love.

it is simply the fascination of being alive.

winter

my heart lifts as we walk together
among the pine trees,
and the wonder is in the wind
breezing through these pine needles
like a benevolent whisper.

we should sit down and write love letters
to the magnificent and magical
that still surrounds us.

if we are awake enough to look,
we can realize that the abundance of wonder
is in our very own backyard.

hurtling toward old age,
i know that my future
will be shorter than my past,
but your impossible beauty
was as clear to me
in that instant of first seeing you
as it has ever been
in all my life of loving you.

we might be invisible to some people,
but not to the ones who matter.

you have made my favorite season winter,
where in this cold weather,
by night and by day
we shelter together,
sharing warmth and memories.

and i remember to give thanks
for something so utterly unexpected.

i know we live on a planet in peril,
but it is still breathtaking
and that is because of you.

my eye-opening
and heart-expanding
daily muse.

existence

having lived at all is an act of consolation.

this improbable miracle of life
as we continue embracing the unknown.

we privileged few
who learned how to love properly,
to write poems,
to make music,
to wrap our arms around each other,
to have extraordinary sensitivity,
and how to cry at the very thought
of leaving you behind.

though my heart is sometimes forlorn,
it is filled with something i cannot name.

i know we all exist
for the briefest moment of time,
but i also know
you have lifted me beyond the everyday.

and in my tireless seeking
for some nobility of being,
it was found in you alone.

hope

if i spend some time in libraries
or bookstores or music stores,
my faith in humanity is restored.

kind of like how the smell of your shampoo
still lingers in the room after your bath.

the question is, can we hold the enormous fragility
and all the suffering that happens simultaneously
and let the scales balance?

do i still have a purpose?

have i contributed anything?

have i provided my children with an ethical kindness?

have i helped those in true need?

i will continue
with this glorious spectacle of life
as you still replenish my whole heart.

the ancient trees

living with the full expression of wakefulness
and with our sensitivity,

we yearn and strive
to make some art,
to make some meaning out of this life.

the ancient trees,
each like a fingerprint,
will save us among the realm of possibility
and the reverence of second chances.

unwrap the love and let it bloom anew
so you are awakened to the delicacy around us.

let us cradle in the arms of the clouds
and the tender waves that curl at our feet.

let love be your every thought and your every feeling
because every single thing we love is irreplaceable.

the affectionate hand you extend is full of generosity,
and your tears will be your emblem of honesty.

be open to uncertainty, because not knowing
can bring you solace, and you can live
with the glory of just being
among the veiling and unveiling of the sun
as we dream together of light and shade.

the beautiful small near misses

opportunities i failed to seize,
happiness i let drift away,
lost chances,
vanished time,
but still, i hold the miracles of every existence.

i am still living life
like a hushed and holy ceremony,
for each moment is a chance to start anew.

i am still aware of how extraordinarily unique
everything really is.

and that only one of each exists:
each parent,
each child,
each love.

it is always **through the heart** where hope lies.

and it is where

every sight we have ever seen,

every touch we have ever touched,

every lip we have ever kissed,

and every love we have ever loved,
still and always will remain.

the sound

the sound of your breathing
is still my favorite lyric
because it gives me time
to gather my prayers and petitions
to this life still filled with
unexpected moments of benevolence
and uncommon splendors of sentiment.

and if there are any moments
that feel unsurvivable,
you will be my gentle guide to a better way.

122 east 76th street, 4th floor

the sun filtered through
the oak tree outside my office,
and i noticed the light
bending around the sun,
and that was all i needed.

and since i'm at work,
what talents do i really have?

i will name a few,
but rest assured these
are most likely not the ones
that the human resources department
and talent development are looking for:

i have a talent
for stillness.

i have a talent
for not forgetting
that to grow old is a tremendous privilege.

i have a talent
for being a broken human being
who has not lost hope.

i have a talent
for weeping daily tears
that are excruciatingly painful
but breathtakingly beautiful.

i have a talent
for knowing that
everything under the sun
is swallowed by darkness in time,

yet i choose to continue.

i have a talent
for holding
a secret sympathy for all.

i have a talent
for acknowledging

the difficult truths,
the endless considerations,
and reconsiderations.

i have a talent
for living the unanswerable questions.

i have a talent
for being defiantly out of step.

i have a talent
for not taking myself too seriously,
but i also have a talent
for taking the noble vocation
of writing poetry very seriously.

i have a talent
for knowing that loss and absence
bring us into all that is here.

i have a talent
for an awareness that all our words matter,
whether an exquisite rarity
or the humblest of battered paperbacks.

i have a talent
for being undone by the final abandonment
yet still resonant with gratitude.

i have a talent
for embracing our deepest states of love
because life is imperfect.

i have a talent
for the singular impressionability of early memory,
which stays with us for life.

i have a talent
to respond by simply putting the book down.

i have a talent
for the sorrow of unmet hope.

i have a talent
for needing less noise

and the deliberate silence of the unsaid.

i have a talent
as a poet because we poets
fall in love and fall apart,
and then fall in love again.

i have a talent
for not networking, not self-promoting,
and not caring about inclusion or attention.

i have a talent
for being vulnerable to despair
and brokenness and yet not losing
the ability to experience life completely.

i have a talent for
staring dreamily
into the distance while offering

an openhearted song
on the conditions of the human heart.

i have a talent
for trembling, bending, breaking,
expanding, and even disappearing.

i have a talent
for making certain my life and love
remain on the edges at all times,
and never the limelight or center stage.

i have a talent
for where my hope lives.

i have a talent
for leaning on these words
when the losses hover over me.

i have a talent
for knowing that
everything is impermanent
and everything changes.

i have a talent
for the remembrance of my father
and how he never expressed

impatience with my questions
or how i saw the world,
and the things i wanted to do,
like writing poetry.

i have a talent
for embracing the enormity
of my mother's boundless love.

i have a talent
for knowing that my brother is my best friend,
and i love him more than words could ever capture.

i have a talent
for dedicating my entire life
to loving my daughters unconditionally.

i have a talent
for understanding that poverty
is never an indication of failure,
it's actually just the opposite sometimes.

i have a talent
for being wrong and
for making terrible
and beautiful mistakes.

i have a talent
for being 1,000 miles from where i was before.

i have a talent
for hearing all that is left to be heard.

i have a talent
to be reminded of your absence,
especially when it rains.

i have a talent
to see how frighteningly capable
we are of ignoring the harm we do to each other.

i have a talent
for not living in a competitive, consumerist society
and purposefully disregarding the status-conscious,
as well as the stress and insecurity this all creates.

i have a talent
to know that a simple kiss can be love.

i have a talent
of being fully aware that i have
more life behind me than ahead of me.

i have a talent
for the enduring resonance of the underappreciated.

i have a talent
for listening to the stories of the worn and the weak.

i have a talent
for failing and stumbling, but trying again.

i have talent
for not striving for achievement at all costs
and never measuring myself by outward success.

i have a talent
for not worshiping intellect over emotion.

i have a talent
for embracing the totality that is life
and the potentiality of living that inhabits
the space between me and my final moments.

i have a talent
for listening to both of my daughters'
breathing during sleep,
which always makes me weep.

i have a talent
for needing the shadows
to illuminate the light so we can see

the radiance all around us.

i have a talent
for not abandoning the little joys
filled with love and kindness.

and i have a talent
for standing in the warm glow of evening,
attempting to capture this human portrayal
of my simple and immense love for you all.

the staggering privilege to live is ours

the brokenhearted belief of our culture of immediacy
and our cult of productivity.

the trance of routine.

we need to stop hiding behind the hours
spent at the office that protect us
so well from the love of life.

i know the secret despair of our busyness.

let's look past the disquieting places and beings
and press daily against the weight of the world
by living with honorable sincerity and large-heartedness.

let's embrace the immeasurability of each human being,
and the light will be revealed where we once saw darkness.

let's go with absolute devotion for something or someone.

let's turn our greatest heartbreak
into our greatest work of art.

let's remember a dream's dissolution
can turn into a seed of possibility.

let's fill our voice with harmony
and pray for everything we lost
when the days of summer grow long and bright.

let's put our finest definition on love,
and the affectionate hand will be extended,
the moon will breathtakingly rise again,
and the whole of life will be reflected in our eyes.

let's make bearable the living testament
of our improbable and finite lives,
because this one life will be its own triumph,
for the staggering privilege to live is ours.

how impossibly beautiful everything really is

i am in midlife now and suffering still,
but just a little.

this has been one of the hardest ones yet.

the scars and attrition,
although a testament to their histories,
have contributed to my visibly vulnerable weathering.

my life remains misunderstood to vulgar eyes,
and it is as it should be.

my inner space is slowly being inhabited
by the daydreamer i knew as a child.

most sleepwalk through;
they are simply too scared
to appreciate the everyday miracles.

the unstudied, undiminished strength of character
has a nice quiet authority of its own;
and they will never know,
and they will never realize,
that all of our moments matter.

it is what makes us who we are,
what makes us worthy of being,
what really counts in the end.

there may be a mournful hint to my eyes,
but it is only because of that now possessed quality
of a little failure and consistent imperfection,
the simple results of an unfinished
but fully lived life.

and now i'm bordering on going completely mad
at how impossibly beautiful everything really is.

postscript

some words that helped ...

For My Dad

A poem by Emma Silich, age 9 [written June 2022]

I love you to the moon and back.

Without you in our world,
I don't know how we would survive.

When I'm feeling down,
you always come to see what's wrong.

When I am sad,
you always make me feel better.

When I am cold,
you get me a blanket or cuddle with me.

When I am scared to go in the ocean,
you go in with me and make me feel better.

You are the best dad.
I would never replace you.

I love you so much.

I don't know how I got such a great father.

I miss you so much on school days
and it breaks my heart when I don't see you.

Thank you for everything.

Thank you for teaching me how to be nice,
and how to love,
and how to stick up for myself.

You are the best.

I love you so much.

Love, Emma

About My Dad

A poem by Mia Silich, age 7 [written October 2022]

My favorite memory of my dad
is when he cuddles with me.

My dad is good at
making furniture and gardening.

My dad always says he loves me
and to please be good to my sister and my mommy.

My dad's favorite thing to eat
is peanut butter and jelly.

My dad is the best dad ever.

My dad is so much fun to hang out with.

My dad is sweet, kind, caring, helpful, and handsome.

I love him so much.

Love, Mia

Acknowlegements

Once again, I would like to thank my publisher, Marina Aris, and the Brooklyn Writers Press for publishing this fifth collection of poetry.

And again, Marina, I want to include this in all my acknowledgements. I thank you for your loyalty and trust, and of course, our over 25-year plus beautiful friendship filled with kindness, tenderness, and understanding.

And for the words you sent me. [April 7, 2024]

"Your words warm my heart, Stephan. I want so much for you to feel validated and appreciated for your work and what you're allowing me to create with you. A true honor."

I would like to thank my editor, Judi Heidel, for her always gentle touch that has provided guidance and inspiration from the first book to this latest.

I would also like to thank my beautiful, inside-and-out, daughters, Emma and Mia. I love you more than anything in this world.

Emma, thank you for the words you sent me on Father's Day. [June 16, 2024]

"You are the best dad ever. I love you so much. I love it when you, Mia and I watch movies together. I also love it when you take us to Starbuck's. I really appreciate it. I also love it when we go to the beach. You are also so good at volleyball, and I love playing with you. I also love it when you cuddle with me. We also find the best comedy movies. I love it when you can't stop laughing. You are a truly inspiring dad. You are my role model. Thank you for always supporting me. I can't wait for all the other memories we are going to make together.

I also love how you don't like to listen to Taylor Swift, but you do for me. I love you so much. I can't wait for the summer. We are going to have so much fun by the pool and by the beach. I can't wait. I also can't wait for us to play in the backyard at East Hampton. I know when you are overprotective, you are just trying to help me and keep me safe. I hope you have a great Father's Day. You are so special to me, and I hope your day is very special because you deserve it. I also really appreciate it when you take us out for food. I know you work very hard every day, and I love you more than anything."

Mia, thank you for the words you sent me on my birthday. [April 30, 2024]

"Dear Daddy, I love you so much. You are the best. Happy Birthday! I hope you have an amazing day. The world is better when you are holding us tight. Since you are a poet here is a poem:

"Roses are red, violets are blue, Daisy's are sweet, and so are you."

You are an amazing dad. I will never ever forget you and how much you love me. I will never forget how much you care about other people. I love you so much. You are so nice. You do so much for me. You are sweet, nice, and funny and sooo handsome. I really hope you know how much I love you."

My Dad, Robert J. Silich, I miss you every minute of every day. And I still feel your presence in everything I do.

Thank you, Dad, for the words you sent me on my 30th birthday:

"You're a wonderful son, and that's why your birthday means so very much. Because it's a day to look back and celebrate all your past accomplishments, a day to look forward and anticipate all your future successes . . . But whatever path you choose, whatever future you make for yourself, know that you are already a success in the eyes of your family. For it has been a great joy to have a son like you to love, to watch grow and mature into a responsible

young man... All that we have shared through the years has only reinforced what a very special person you are and how deserving you are of life's best. Happy Birthday, Son. I love you. Life is just beginning. —Pop"

My Mom, Dianne Silich. There are no words to describe how much I love you.

Thank you, Mom for the words you sent me. [June 14, 2024]

"Stephan - you deserve only the best. You are so worthy. Be strong. You are the best person I know. You are so kind and caring - perhaps too much. Hang in there. I love you. Mom."

My brother, Robert C Silich, the closest person to me and the most supportive and compassionate human being I know. Like I said before, you are the only person I have ever looked up to and the only true gentleman I know. Thank you for inspiring and sustaining me. I love you.

Thank you, Rob, for the words you sent me on my first day of law school back in 1992:

"You'll never know what it's like to look up to younger brother. I can't remember when it happened. You are the hero, the protector, and the standard for me. Just remember that no matter how bad it gets, that outside the lecture room window, across the quadrangle, on the other side of Massachusetts Avenue, is the real world where people live, die, love and hate each minute of every day. In my short time in medicine, I've seen young people as well as old, die and become ill – no one is excused from mortality . . . love as much as you can in our brief time here. A quiz, a test, an exam, a course, a semester, a year, a degree, a career – 'in the end, the love you take is equal to the love you make.' No matter what you do, or what kind of lawyer you become (gasp!?), or even if you don't become a lawyer, remember this only: You have only one mother, one father, and one brother, it's very simple – one of each makes it easy to love. I love you and always will of course – no matter what. You are the brightest star in my life. and that's that. Peace, brother. Love, Robert."

My grandmother, Greta Silich, and for the words she wrote me June 21, 1995:

"Stephan dear, I am writing just to say, 'I love you' and I wanted to ask you whether or not you fancy foreign films. The particular film is Italian with English subtitles. The title is 'Il Postino.' The reviews were raves. It deals with everyday living and stresses the importance of poetry. Whatever you decide I felt the film would interest you, especially because you write such beautiful words. With great love always. – Nana xo."

My grandmother, Pauline "Nana" Ray, and my grandfather, Chester "Pops" Ray for their words on November 29, 1988:

"Dear Stephan, Enclosed you will find this photo of Pops and I. I gave one to each of you, in the hopes that when you look at us, you will realize that we love you all so much, and want the best for you, as we are very proud of every one of you. When we see the kind of people in our society it makes us realize how very blessed, we are in having such beautiful grandchildren of whom we are so proud of. Stephan, reading the papers, I came across this article which I enclosed – you are so good at poetry, I figured you should send in an entry – you are so talented when it comes to words and express your heart and feelings so well. So many of your poems you wrote were beautiful – try your luck! I love you more than you will ever know! Hope to see you all at Christmas. Take care. All our love, Nana and Pops."

My Aunt Grace who wrote these words on April 30th, 1989:

"My dearest Stephan, Hope with all my heart that you enjoy the Happiest of Birthdays!! Remember to fully enjoy each second, sweetie. Have the most wonderful New Year!! You're in my thoughts, most loving, and ever in my prayers. Don't forget to 'kick up your heels' and tell the powers that be: 'Oh, what a marvelous time I'm enjoying'. Always the best of happiness and love!! Your ever most loving Aunt Grace."

Thank you, Jennifer Fontao, for the words you wrote on April 30, 2024:

"Happy blessed and blissful birthday, my dear Stephan. What an incredible feeling I hold in my heart today as we celebrate you in the world. You have become my best friend, and I don't say that lightly. It's my truth. I don't know anyone like you, and I am always learning because of you. This birthday is so meaningful, and it marks such an uphill climb. In this life, you have truly traveled bravely - living on your own terms and the reward of that integrity is your truth, awareness, and most of all: purpose. You have many wonderful stories (both good and bad) which have shaped, twisted and turned your take on being! And what an incredible being you are. I am often in awe at how unique and humble you show up, especially with that killer smile and head of hair. But seriously, I know how difficult and vulnerable this year has been for you, and for all that I love you so and I am just so overwhelmed with joy and love for you today on your birthday. I celebrate you with all the beauty my heart can hold. Jennifer"

Father Lux from Xavier High School who wrote these words September 26, 1986:

"Dear Stephan, This is a letter that I very much want to write and yet in my personal shyness I find it hard to tell you all that I want to say to you. Anyway, I will put that aside and do it. Stephan, you are a young man whom I watched grow through my own eyes, but perhaps through the eyes of our mutual friend – Father David Ciancimino. Dave is a man I love and respect very much and he speaks so highly of your character. I personally enjoy what I believe is your affection for Mr. Curley, our literature professor, and your work on the Literary Magazine. Everyone raves about your eloquent words. I feel privileged to have heard about that horrible accident you witnessed with the mother's death in front of her family while taking your brother to Georgetown. Please know that you are living in a very special private and privileged time and can only hope that you realize the lord's incredible love for you and pride in you. I pray that you enjoy this time together and also enjoy this time with your family and friends. Please know that I pray for you in a special way each day and know that I love you and wish you very well. With affection and devotion, Father Lux."

For the others, the very few others, you always know who you are, and I love you.

About the Author

Stephan Silich, an award-winning poet and storyteller, masterfully interweaves art, literature, and the diverse landscapes of New York's iconic streets. His collections seamlessly blend vibrant and mundane moments of lived experience with the intricacies of human emotion, crafting a rich lyrical tapestry that resonates deeply with poetry lovers.

Born into a family of healers, Silich's work is infused with a profound sense of compassion and empathy. His father, a surgical oncologist, his mother, a pediatric nurse, and his brother, a plastic and reconstructive surgeon, all influenced his unique perspective on the human experience.

Silich's journey as a writer began at 13, inspired by his parents' encouragement and shaped by his brother Robert's advice:

"If it sounds like writing, then rewrite it. Sometimes your poetry is the victim of poetry. Just write from your heart and the words will beautifully arrive."

This counsel has guided Silich's approach, resulting in critically acclaimed collections that speak directly to the heart.

His debut, *The Silence Between What I Think and What I Say* (2018), earned praise from Kirkus Reviews.

"Silich slips effortlessly into a long tradition of New York poets from Walt Whitman to Frank O'Hara and his poems are a delight."

—Kirkus

His second collection, *Tonight Will Be the Longest Night of Them All*, was a finalist in the prestigious 2021 Next Generation Independent Book Awards. Subsequent collections, *Putting the Trembling Kiss at Ease* (2023) and *Remember Me as a Time of Day* (2024), also received critical acclaim and have further cemented his reputation for evocative and lyrical prose.

Praised for over two decades for his vulnerability and contemplative candor, Silich's work offers a unique form of poetic medicine that soothes the soul and mends the spirit. His blend of memoir and introspection invites poetry lovers to explore how human emotions and human experience converge. Many of his devoted readers claim his perspective on the recurring themes in his work, namely: family, love, loss, art, literature, and creative muses, such as his native New York have transformed them.

Silich divides his time between Manhattan and East Hampton, where he lives with his two daughters, Emma and Mia. He continues to write daily, with several collections in progress, solidifying his place as a significant voice in contemporary American poetry.

THANK YOU FOR READING

How Impossibly Beautiful Everything Really Is
by Stephan Silich

If you enjoyed this book, please consider leaving a review on Goodreads or your preferred platform. Your feedback supports quality content and helps inspire future releases.

Connect with Stephan Silich

@stephan_silich

Want the latest from the Brooklyn Writers Press?
Browse our complete catalog

brooklynwriterspress.com

www.ingramcontent.com/pod-product-compliance
Lightning Source LLC
Chambersburg PA
CBHW040251090526
44586CB00041B/2748